Drafting and Editing

——— Richard Andrews ———

UNWIN HYMAN
SKILLS AND RESOURCES SERIES

Published in 1990 by
UNWIN HYMAN LIMITED
15/17 Broadwick Street
London W1V 1FP

British Library Cataloguing in Publication Data
Andrews, Richard
    Drafting and editing.
    1. Secondary schools. Curriculum subjects: English literature. Texts. Editing techniques.
        Questions & answers.
    I. Title
808.02

ISBN 0-04-448106-3

Designed by Bob Wright and Ann Nimmo
Illustrated by Peter Kent
Typeset by Acūté Design, Stroud, Glos.
Printed in Great Britain by The Alden Press Limited, Oxford
Bound by Hunter & Foulis Limited

Acknowlegements

My co-author on *From Rough to Best*, John Noble, was responsible with me for the conception behind that book, and I am grateful to him not only for that initial collaboration, but also for the material he and Lonely Planet Publications supplied for this book. I would also like to thank John Greenwood, photographer, for his photographs and interest; Mark Wilford and Shaun Sutton of *The Beverley Guardian*; the English subject officers at the five GCSE examining boards; James Berry, Sylvia Emerson; Lorraine Gormally, Hazel Hutchinson and their pupils at Cottinghan School, Hull; Phil Jarrett and Adele; Hemlata Joshi, Tessa McInnerny, Victoria Burgess, Hugo de Burgh and Julia Kim for their poems from *Typhoon*, literary magazine of Island School, Hong Kong; Jimmy, a pupil of mine George Green's School, Isle of Dogs, London; Michael Simons and John Stephens of The English Centre, London; and James Berry for permission to reprint his story 'Becky and the Wheels-and brake Boys'.

The author and publishers would like to thank the following for permission to reproduce extracts and illustrations in the pupils' pages:

Beverley street plan reproduced with the permission of C.J. Utting   (10)
'Back and Forth' and 'Invincible' © The Sunday Telegraph Ltd   (11)
Charles Vyse Associates for 'Go Turkey' from Sunmed Summer 1989   (13)
'Man flees naked from house to raise alarm' report by courtesy of the *Sevenoaks Chronicle*   (26)
Hamish Hamilton Ltd for 'Becky and the Wheels-and-Brake Boys' by James Berry from *A Thief in the Village* by James Berry copyright ©, 1987   (28B)
The Beverley Guardian for 'Mercy flight'   (29A), 'Call to remove age limit on drinks'   (29B) and 'A close shave for hospital'   (30)
John Calder (Publishers) Ltd, London for *Exercises in Style* by Raymond Queneau and translated by Barbara Wright, © Editions Gallimard 1947, translation © Barbara Wright 1958, 1979   (32A)
John Greenwood for extract on Illumineering   (40)
Forbes Shire Council, New South Wales for 'Gentleman thief?'   (41A)

Contents

Unit	Key stage	Details	Approx. Time
1 Plan it!	3/4	*Making plans:* working from initial ideas to fully fledged plans.	1 hr
2 Looking at instructions	3	*Informative writing 1:* writing instructions and carrying them out.	1 hr
3 Follow that guide!	3/4	*Informative writing 2:* writing a manual – sequencing instructions, awareness of audience.	2 hrs
4 A poet's-eye view	3	*Poems 1:* following the development of a poem from lists to drafts to the completed work.	1½–2 hrs
5 A tiny problem	3	*Letters:* reading a text critically with a view to editing it down and clarifying it. Writing instructions in a letter.	1 hr
6 Once upon a time . . .	3/4	*Narrative 1:* arranging photographs in a narrative sequence; writing a story based on this sequence.	2 hrs
7 Poetry choice	3/4	*Poems 2:* Selecting poems for an anthology; writing a report justifying the selection.	1½ hrs
8 Picture it!	3/4	*Looking at photographs:* selecting pictures for a purpose, sequencing, judging audience; writing captions and headlines.	1½ hrs

Unit	Key Stage	Details	Approx. Time
9 Pen-friends?	3	*Collaborative writing:* writing a playscript for performance on tape or live.	1 week
10 Giving directions	3	*Informative writing 3:* giving directions, working in pairs.	1 hr
11 Putting it in a nutshell	3	*Mini-sagas:* writing to a word limit; editing for a precise form.	1hr
12 It all began . . .	3/4	*Narrative 2:* selection; trying different structures and sequencing in writing; connecting image and word.	2 hrs+
13 Going places	3/4	*Brochure 1:* using synonyms and antonyms; writing in a persuasive style.	1½ hrs
14 A first class poem?	3	*Poems 3:* collaborative composition of stanzas; combining these into a poem.	1 hr
15 Paper-chase poem	3	*Poems 4:* composition of a poem from a given jumble of single lines.	45 mins
16 Have you read. . .?	3	*Blurbs:* writing in a persuasive and informative style for a special purpose.	1 hr
17 Have a closer look	3/4	*Focussing on detail 1:* descriptive writing; including detail.	1–1½ hrs

Unit	Key Stage	Details	Approx. Time
18 Action time!	3/4	*Focussing on detail 2:* expanding descriptive texts.	1 hr
19 Here is the news	3	*Television news:* sequencing news items.	1 hr
20 Rough stuff	3	*Subediting 1:* initial practice in subediting texts.	45 mins to 1 hr
21 Focus on spelling	3/4	*Subediting 2:* practice in checking spelling in texts.	45 mins
22 Focus on sentence structure	3/4	*Subediting 3:* checking sentence structure and punctuation.	45 mins
23 Short and sweet!	3/4	*Subediting 4:* rewriting over-elaborate language.	45 mins
24 Putting your ideas in order	3/4	*Argument:* sequencing the paragraphs of an essay.	45 mins
25 Headline news	3/4	*Report 1:* writing a newspaper report based on given notes; writing a headline.	1½ hrs
26 The bare facts	3/4	*Summary:* reducing a given newspaper article to a summarised version.	1 hr

Unit	Key Stage	Details	Approx. Time
27 Story-time	3/4	*From storytelling to story writing:* telling, recording and transcribing stories; producing a written version.	1 week
28 Behind the scenes	3/4	*From story to script:* searching out dialogue and using it as the basis for a script; translating narrative into scene-setting and dialogue.	1 week
29 Going national!	3/4	*Report 2:* rewriting a local newspaper story for a national paper; editing, summarising, rewriting.	1–1½ hrs
30 Editorial changes	3/4	*Report 3:* discussion of drafts; head-line writing.	45 mins
31 Getting into print	4	*Travel writing:* editing a narrative draft for an informative text.	1–1½ hrs
32 A matter of style!	4	*Style:* rewriting the same text in a variety of styles.	2 hrs
33 Tell me about it	3/4	*Interviews 1:* simulated interviews in class.	1 hr
34 Meeting point	4	*Interviews 2:* conducting interviews outside the classroom.	1 week

Unit	Key Stage	Details	Approx. Time
35 **Think about your readers**	3/4	*Rewriting for younger children:* changing style and content for a new audience.	1 hr+
36 **A very strange case**	3/4	*Solving a mystery:* working from evidence; writing a report or story or list.	2 hrs
37 **Selling off the page**	4	*Brochure 2:* writing a company brochure.	1½ hrs
38 **Time for order**	4	*Report 4:* handling time shifts in report writing and narrative.	2 hrs
39 **Dotting the 'i's**	4	*Copy editing:* improving poor writing – paragraphing, sentence structure, style, spelling.	1 hr
40 **The art of selling**	3/4	*Brochure 3:* designing, writing and presenting a brochure.	2 hrs
41 **Who was Ben Hall?**	4	*Eliminating bias:* writing a neutral account using facts extracted from two biased acccounts.	1–1½ hrs
42 **Ways of working**	3/4	*Wordprocessing:* discussion of the pros and cons of this technique.	45 mins
43 **Hold the front page!**	3/4	*Newspapers: the front page* – collaborative work on design and writing.	1 week

Teachers' Guide

Background

In the early eighties, John Noble of *The Observer* and I wrote a book called *From Rough to Best*. As journalist/ sub-editor and teacher/writer, we wanted to produce a book for schools that drew on the editing practices in newspapers, in photography, in film and in the production of other written texts, and which applied them to the business of writing in schools.

For all the strengths of that book – which in many ways (without our knowing it at the time) reflected concerns and interests in writing research–with hindsight, we would have changed much of it. One of its weaknesses was that it focussed rather too much on the 'surface features' of language: on sentence structure, spelling, style and punctuation. There was still the feeling that some of the assignments were too like 'exercises'.

Drafting and Editing attempts to redress some of these imbalances, and, in particular, focusses more on the structural aspects of composition and less on the surface elements. It is based on the premise that the skills of drafting and editing (terms that were not current in schools, even in the early eighties) are useful ones to acquire, and that they are best acquired in the service of writing or talk that is compelling in itself, or is impelled by some demand, issue, idea or imaginative drive generated by the student.

Drafting is a term that covers everything from making initial plans for a piece of writing to producing versions of the writing that have not yet reached final form. It is close in nature to what went on in what used to be called 'rough' books (with all the unfortunate connotations that 'rough' carried with it): and also to what goes on in writers' notebooks – which is often meticulously crafted. It has acquired more status in the writing process, because it is understood to be a stage (or series of stages) in which the writer makes crucial decisions about the shaping of what he or she wants to say.

Rewriting and *revision* tend to be distinguished according to the scale of the reworking: rewriting often implies a major review of content and structure, whereas revision suggests a reworking and fine tuning of an existing content and structure. Revision, however, as the term itself hints, can be far more radical than a mere tinkering with the surface features of a text. One of the aims of this book is to help students reconsider the content and structure of their work in the light of the purpose and audience of their writing.

Editing, as far as writing in the classroom is concerned, is a broader term than perhaps has been acknowledged. Editors (of newspapers, books, anthologies, films) have a crucial role to play, not only in checking and revising text where necessary and in preparing these texts for production, but also in the actual making of the text. They may advise on content and selection, and most certainly will advise on structure and form. Far from playing a narrowly *critical* role, their contribution to the final outcome of the text is essentially *creative* too. Another of the aims of this book is to help students to enact the role of editor, both in groups in the classroom and also in their own heads.

Basic principles

Interest in the *process* of writing (often at the expense of the product) has grown in the last ten years, and in the USA has become something of an epidemic. What can we glean from this growth in interest that can be useful to students learning to write, and useful to us as teachers helping them to learn?

It is probably fair to say that drafting is a common practice for writers: not only for writers of 'literary' material but also for writers of advertising copy, minutes of meetings, press releases, business letters, applications, and so on. This does not mean to say that everyone does it every time they write something: the drafting of a note, memo, personal letter (except in exceptional circumstances) or list (unless it had to be revised) would seem neurotic. The point is that whenever the role of the written text *as text* (i.e. medium as well as message) is important, or when precision counts, it pays to draft your text first to ensure that you do say what you want to say.

The method of work which distinguishes 'rough' and 'best' work from drafting is different because the early versions of composition in drafting are given more status, and may well be the main focus of the teacher's attention. Previously, 'rough' books were mostly used only by the students, and were rarely discussed with peers or the teacher.

The advantages of the teacher or fellow-students intervening during the writing process rather than after it (in 'marking' a finished piece of written work, for example) are clear: the writer is more likely to want to change and improve his or her work-in-progress than make alterations once the work is deemed to be 'finished'. Such is the nature of much school writing that it is seen as a 'task' or 'assignment', and when the writer sees it as 'finished', he or she 'downs tools'. Intervention during the writing process, on the other hand, means that student and teacher are working together to produce a piece of writing that is appropriate to its function and audience.

Drafting also allows attention to be focussed on specific aspects of writing at *different* stages of the writing act: on the subject matter, on the style or register (and thus on the audience), on the overall structure, on the position of the writer in relation to his or her material (person, tone, mood, etc.), and on the accuracy of the grammatical constructions, on the punctuation, on the spelling, on the layout, on the handwriting – and so on. Conventional practice often attempted to address all of these elements at the same time, conflating what Frank Smith in *Writing and the Writer* calls the compositional and secretarial aspects of writing. No wonder that many of our weaker students found (or more depressingly, find) this approach unhelpful.

In summary, then, drafting and editing are useful practices in that:
● they give the student time to work out exactly what he or she wants to say;

● they separate compositional from secretarial stages in writing;
● they make the student more aware of the writing process;
● they make the teacher more aware of the writing process, and enable the teacher to intervene at the most productive stage of composition.

Two examples

1 The drafting and editing of a piece of writing do not always mean that the finished piece will be shorter and more concise than the first draft. In the drafts shown here, by Helen Rimmer, a 6-year-old working on a wordprocessor (see introductory notes on page 5 and Unit 42), the principle behind the revisions is one of *expansion*. You might like to discuss the nature of the revisions in Helen's work. These were carried out largely without the help of a teacher.

1 I am playing on my roller boots.they are new roller boots. I play with my friend Anna. Anna has some roller boots. my roller boots are sipre.

2 I am playing on my roller boots. they are new roller boots. I play with my friend Anna. Anna has some roller boots. my roller boots are sipre. I fell down on my roller boots.I cut my leg.I went home and my mummy wiped my leg. I went back to play with my friend Anna. after we had a little play my mum cried "Helen". I had to go in. I had to get ready for bed.

3 I natud and natud for some roller boots. one day we went to town. my mum said to my dad lets go to by some roller boots we went to a toy shop. I am playing on my roller boots. I play with my friend Anna. Anna has some roller boots. my roller boots are sipre. I fell down on my roller boots.I cut my leg.I went home and my mummy wiped my leg. I went back to play with my friend Anna. after we had a little play my mum cried "Helen". I had to go in. when I got in I said "mum can I have another minit?" my mum said "yes".I went back to play with Anna after a little play I had to go in. I had to get ready for bed.

4 my roller boots

I nattered and nattered for some roller boots. one day we went to town. my mum said to my dad "let's go to buy some roller boots". we went to a toy shop. I am playing on my roller boots. I play with my friend Anna. Anna has some roller boots. my roller boots are slippery. I fell down on my roller boots.I cut my leg.I went home and my mummy wiped my leg. I went back to play with my friend Anna. after we had a little play my mum cried "Helen". I had to go in. when I got in I said "mum can I have another minute?" my mum said "Yes".I went back to play with Anna.after a little play I had to go in. I had to get ready for bed.

2 The following drafts were composed in a first-year, mixed-ability class in a comprehensive school in Yorkshire. The class had been asked to put themselves in the shoes of children evacuated from London to the countryside in the Second World War. These were first drafts. Putting yourself in the role of teacher of this class, what would you say to each of the students as you discuss the work with them?

The original drafts, which were handwritten, were not available for reproduction here. Various crossings out and alterations are omitted.

> *Strange un-friendly faces peer at me from behind*
> *unknown doors.*
> *I here Whispers in an eerie language.*
> *A new room with a new view.*
> *Shunned by strongly accented children.*
>
> *Wandering empty pocketed and alone*
> *Peering in at sweet shop wonders, dreaming of the taste*
> *of my favourite sweets.*
> *Aimlessly climbing trees and worrying about my family*
> *The emptiness of my stomach lightened only slightly by*
> *meagre and sparse meals.*
> *Lying in my cold bed I wonder how long I will have*
> *to stay here*
> *Cows and chickens seen only in pictures walk freely*
> *around me.*
> *Filled by rain streams chuckle and gurgle from the hills.*
> *Everywhere I am watched by cold and dreary mountain*
> *Cold, lonely and homesick*

> *They are two children in the*
> *farm with me They are both*
> *my friends*
>
> *I quite like this place because they*
> *are lots of dens to go in*
>
> *The accomadation is great*
> *we get good meals and a room each*
>
> *I sometimes see war planes go by*
>
> *I miss my parents very much*
> *The people who look after me are*

Notes   [5]The children here.   [2]The family.   [1]Your family.   [4]The school.

[6]The food.   [3]The strange place.

1st draft   *I miss my family while I'm here,*
But the Joneses are very kind and they accepted me.
The house is old and the farm is wide.
The smell of the cows and pigs are vile
And the fields are heavily manured.

At school the children run wild
And no teacher stops them.
Education is poor here but it is not as bad as the school.
The school is an old pub and it's soon going to be demolished.

I'm missing my family and their cooking
Because here we only have cheese, poultry and bread.
The rashions are scarce and fuel is low
And I miss my friends, my best pals.
For kids here are Welsh speakers only and they won't make friends.

2nd draft   *I'm missing my family and home*
But the Joneses are very kind to me I like it here.
The old farmhouse is warm and cheery.
Though the vile stench of animals ruin the atmosphere.

School is miserable and I think the kids haven't seen soap.
Teachers don't teach much,
School is full of rumours and the school's a pub.

The role of the teacher

Introducing drafting into the classroom changes the relation of the teacher to the work produced by the students, and, of course, the relationship between the teacher and the students as writers. Instead of being a kind of critic who looks at work after it has been finished, evaluating it with a mark (out of 10 or 20 or on some grade basis), or with a comment ('Good work!' 'Good, but take care with your paragraphs.' 'I really enjoyed this piece Karl. You have combined a sensitivity to language with a strong story-line, and the result is an excellent folk-tale.'), the teacher stands alongside the writer as he or she composes, giving advice and coaching, and setting up collaborations between students which will help the individual writers to see the development of their own work more clearly.

Discussing the students' work in class, either as you move around the class or at your desk, is one way to do this. Discussion need not take the form of the teacher pointing out where the writer could improve his or her work. It could (perhaps should?) take the form of asking the writer what his/her intention is, whether he/she is happy with progress so far and, more specifically, whether he/she feels the beginning is right, whether what has been written is really what is intended, and so on. Donald Graves and his co-researchers in the late seventies and early eighties coined the term 'conferencing' for this practice. (See Graves, *Writing: Children and teachers at work*, Heinemann, London 1983.)

Much of Graves' work was carried out with primary school children so there would have been time for such negotiation. In the secondary English classroom time is at more of a premium and it would be impossible to give each child such attention, even within a double period. Because of this, discussions *between* students can be very useful, particularly regarding questions of intention, structure, audience (i.e. the broader compositional questions).

Another way for the teacher to intervene during the writing process is for him or her to 'take in' the work for a detailed appraisal during its composition. The responses to the students' work can be written in the margins of the drafts and given to the writers, who will take action based upon the suggestions. Remember that in conventional practice, the students take very little action when they 'get their work back', other than to carry out decontextualised 'corrections'.

It is in looking closely at students' work in draft form that the teacher can gain an insight into the strengths and weaknesses of the individual student's writing. This involves detailed record-keeping, and also allows the teacher to analyse what Mina Shaughnessy (*in Errors and Expectations*, Oxford University Press, New York 1977), Gunther Kress (in *Learning to Write*, Routledge & Kegan Paul, London 1982) and others call the 'logic of error' in children's work. Analysis of these patterns can form the basis of decisions about which action to take next in helping the individual child to progress.

But what about the 'secretarial' dimension to writing, the area in which most critical response to children's work has traditionally been focussed? We can define this dimension as comprising sentence structure, punctuation, spelling and handwriting or typing.

There are various approaches we can take here. The most teacher-directed one is to do all the 'correcting' for the student on the draft, and have the student incorporate these changes as he or she 'writes up' the piece in a final version. Although this approach may be marginally preferable to decontextualised spelling or 'grammar' exercises, it doesn't ask much of the student, and it is not permitted if work is to be entered for assessment in GCSE coursework folders.

Its one advantage, perhaps, is that it can help a weak student to produce an accurate finished product which in turn may give him or her confidence to pursue the business of learning to write.

At the other extreme, the student takes full responsibility for polishing the work. He or she can be asked to check these surface features and to attempt to produce as perfect a text as possible. Teacher-intervention is usually limited to pointing out where certain inaccuracies are but letting the student solve these for himself or herself; or – in the case of spelling, for example – directing the student to spelling rules and patterns that will help solve the particular problems.

Talk and writing

It has been implicit so far that talk has a large role to play in the making of written pieces of work in the classroom. Many of the units included in this book exploit the opportunities available in the classroom for students to talk with each other about completed texts, or about the composition of written texts. In collaborative writing, for example, talk is essential. A group of three students working together to make a script for performance on tape will need to:

- plan the theme, characters and plot of the scene, and if they are to write in role, decide who is going to take which part;
- read out the script as they compose it, discussing what is going to come next as well as the exact wording of the speeches;
- decide whether each should write longer speeches (perhaps for homework), and on completion of these, discuss how to integrate them into the existing script;
- review the whole scene, and revise where appropriate;
- rehearse a reading of the script, working toward. . .
- . . . the final performance.

They could even, given editing facilities on the tape recorder, discuss how to edit the recorded version and, still further, review the whole project from inception to final performance.

But a text need not be written collaboratively in order to involve talk. When texts are produced by individual students, there is still plenty of scope for talk at the various stages of production: in planning, in the early stages of shaping the text, in reflecting on the intention and direction of the piece, in discussing structure, in checking surface details, and so on. This workshop approach to composing makes the most of the social dimension to writing that schools and classrooms offer.

Using drafting and editing sparingly

Both drafting and editing are techniques that can be helpful in learning to write and in producing written texts. They are not a panacea for all problems in the learning and teaching of writing, and should be introduced with judgement.

For a start, not all writing occasions lend themselves to drafting as a preliminary to the production of the actual text. As was pointed out at the beginning of this introduction, notes, memos, personal letters, lists and other such forms of writing hardly warrant a draft (though there are occasions when each of these forms will demand at least two versions).

More important as far as the classroom is concerned is that the practice of drafting and editing must not be followed slavishly. Its strength is that it reflects a certain theory of the way we bring texts into being: that these are planned, framed loosely and gradually acquire definition. But it is essential to remember that the actual practice of producing a text need not follow the assumed course of its evolution.

Some writers in our classrooms have already internalised the drafting and editing model of composing, and find going through the stages outlined above unnecessary. To enforce such an approach would be to cramp those writers' methods. Writers like this are often highly competent at structuring language in the head, and in many ways are the kind of writers we would like to see emerging from schooling. They remind us that drafting and editing are means to an end, not ends in themselves.

Other writers may find the business of reworking a piece of writing a frustrating activity. It is well worth recalling James Britton's observation (in 'Shaping at the point of utterance', *Learning to Write: First Language, Second Language*, ed Freedman, Pringle and Yalden; Longman, Harlow 1983) that 'Once a writer's words appear on the page, I believe they act primarily as a stimulus to continuing – to further writing, that is, and not primarily as a stimulus to rewriting.'

Wordprocessing

Before we consider the effect that wordprocessors have on the way we write, let us take into account the poet Charles Causley's reaction to Brian Merrick's question (in *Talking with Charles Causley*, NATE Publications 1989):

BM You don't type and you don't use a word-processor?

CC Oh no! Never use anything like that. That's absolute death! If you type – this is even true of the difficult business of writing prose, which I do as little as possible – if you type something it looks too good too quickly. The manuscript should be an absolute mess, and then when you come to type it up and start correcting it from that, if it looks as if it reads pretty well in that

CC awful mess, it is going to look OK when you put it into type.

This in itself is evidence of a poet drafting and editing his work ('The manuscript should be an absolute mess'), but what he says about the word-processor is worth noting. There is the danger that writing will 'look too good too quickly', disguising lack of quality in fine presentation.

There are other pitfalls and constraints in using a wordprocessor. One is the size of the screen, which rarely matches the size of paper one would want to compose on. Some people find that they need space around the edge of the text, both in order to see the shape of the text more easily, and to write annotations and extra text. This element of *space* in the making of texts is not often considered.

Another disadvantage is that unless hard copies (printouts) of the text are made at each stage of the revision process, it is difficult to keep a record of the evolution of a text. Although one can argue that keeping a record of drafts is not necessary, there are occasions when having access to such records is important: if a student produces wordprocessed work at home for instance, and always arrives with perfect copy, how are we as teachers to find out how the work came about?

Third, there is the question of access. Writing on paper can be carried out virtually anywhere. Fourth, you need basic keyboard skills in order to wordprocess.

And yet it is not coincidental that the advent of the wordprocessor has taken place at about the same time as the rise in the interest in drafting. In many ways, wordprocessing enables writers to pay more attention to the nature of their emergent work than before, simply because editing is easier and faster than with pen and paper.

The ability to move paragraphs around is one of the most important facilities. It is not possible to do this when writing or typewriting without reworking the entire piece, but a wordprocessor allows the structure of a piece of writing to be altered easily. It is possible to experiment with alternative structures before deciding which one suits the purpose best. But the point must be noted that the wordprocessor does not tell the writer what to move and where to move it to: this is still in the hands of the writer – hence (partly) the need for this book.

Similarly, at the level of the sentence, it is possible to delete and add words with the minimum of fuss. At the word level, spellings can be corrected, either by the writer unaided or with the help of a spellchecker. But spellcheckers themselves have drawbacks: although most of them are able to identify most mis-spelt words, the alternative suggestions they make are often crudely based on the first string of letters in the misspelt word. They have problems with proper nouns. They certainly do not replace a mind puzzling its way to solving a problem, and they cannot be relied upon to help poor spellers to improve.

The national curriculum

The Cox Report (*English 5–16: Proposals of the Secretary of State for Education and Science and the Secretary of State for Wales,* HMSO June 1989) is clear in its recommendations on the programmes of study for writing. As well as being able to write in different forms for different purposes and audiences, to write coherently about a wide range of topics, and to craft writing which is significantly different from speech (all of which are embodied in the units in this book), the Report states that pupils should
> *know when and how to plan, draft, redraft, revise and proof-read their work* (17.15)

and furthermore, that
> *pupils should keep in their files the necessary range and variety of types of writing, including where appropriate any rough notes, plans or early drafts.* (17.18)

Drafting and editing enter the attainment targets at **level 3,** where pupils should be able to
> *begin to revise and redraft in discussion with the teacher, other adults, or other children in class, paying attention to meaning and clarity as well as checking for matters such as correct and consistent use of tenses and pronouns.*

At **level 4,** they should be able to
> *attempt independent redrafting and revision of their own writing and talk about changes they have made.*

By **level 5,** to
> *assemble ideas on paper, or on a computer screen, or in discussion with others, and show some ability to produce a draft from them and then to redraft and revise as necessary;*

and at **level 7,** to
> *show an increased awareness that a first draft is malleable, e.g. by changing the form in which the material is cast, or by moving text around (either on paper or on a computer screen) or by altering sentence structure or choice of vocabulary.* (17.34)

There is also full provision for the inclusion of drafting and editing in the national curriculum under attainment targets 4 and 5: spelling and presentation, e.g. at **level 3:**
> *In revising and redrafting their writing* pupils should be able to] *begin to check the accuracy of their spelling* (17.35)

and by **level 6,** they should be able to
> *check final drafts of writing for misspellings, using a dictionary or computer spelling checker when appropriate* (17.37)

Finally, under the general provisions for key stage 3, the report suggests that
> *pupils should begin to learn explicitly the different stages in the writing process, i.e. drafting (getting ideas on to paper or computer screen, regardless of*

form, organisation or expression); redrafting (shaping and structuring the raw material – either on paper or on screen – to take account of purpose, audience and form); re-reading and revising (making alterations that will help the reader, e.g. getting rid of ambiguity, vagueness, incoherence, or irrelevance); proof-reading (checking for errors, e.g. omitted or repeated words, mistakes in spelling and punctuation).

All of the techniques just described are the subject of this book. Via this statement from the section of the Cox Report on 'Assessment in secondary school' (17.65), they lead us on to the next part of this introduction:

> *In both key stages 3 and 4 [pupils] should have the opportunity to present an extended piece of work that has been planned, drafted, revised and polished over a period of time.*

Drafting, editing and formal assessments

As coursework has established itself in the last ten years, and particularly since the changes in assessment method brought to the fore by GCSE and the National Curriculum, the question of the role of drafting and editing in the production of assignments has been raised. The basic position of most examination boards is represented by this statement from one of the syllabuses:

> *redrafting is permitted as part of the teaching process. However, it is not permissible to mark intensively [on drafts] so that fair copies can be written up for presentation. Where significant redrafting has taken place, the fact should be noted on the submitted piece and the original draft may be attached for reference.*

This means in general that help given in the normal teaching situation, like advice about structure, the appropriateness of intention to form, and other 'macro' issues is permissible, but that to 'correct' any of the surface features of the text (sentence structure, spelling, etc.) would breach the informal contract between student, teacher and examining board.

Making the distinction between what is and what is not permissible is not always easy, and it is advisable to consult your examining board to make sure exactly where you stand. Broadly speaking, attention should be directed at the content and structural features of the work at draft stage, and proof-reading be reserved for your response to the final piece submitted for the folder. The boards are primarily interested in writing as product, though they are anxious for teachers to record the contexts within which the products are created.

What is heartening about such a situation – both for formal assessment and lower down the school – is that the teacher is freed from the unproductive and time-wasting practice of marking as proof-reading, in order to spend more time at the structural, generic level of the process in collaboration with the students.

How to use this book

The last point indicates the direction in which this book, and the units contained within it, are heading. This isn't a book which teaches a set of discrete 'skills' in a vacuum, which in turn it is hoped will be applied to any writing situation. Rather, it aims to provide activities – both in talk and in writing – which will draw on and develop the ability to take control of texts. Gaining command of the language in this way is an important 'skill' to acquire, because it enables the student not only to write with more power and range (through a widening of the repertoire and the seeing of possible alternatives to framing a particular piece of writing) but to read more incisively as well.

The units are arranged in order of complexity, so it is possible to start at the beginning and over a year (or five years) work through them. Needless to say, however, development in language competence is not along a simple linear track, and it might be a better approach to employ these units at appropriate moments in the course of work at key stages 3 and 4 and beyond.

To this end, the contents pages at the front of the book list the units and provide a brief note as to the aims and objectives of each. This summary is supplemented by the teachers' notes, which follow this introduction and give a much fuller rationale and methodology for each of the units.

A final point

Karel Reisz, the film director, has stated that 'the process of editing is the crucial act in the production of a film'. He went on to give an example:

> *If one were to join a shot of a smiling actor to a close shot of a revolver, and follow this with another shot of the actor, now terrified, the total impression of the sequence would be to suggest that the actor was behaving in a cowardly manner. If, on the other hand, the two shots of the actor were reversed, the audience would see the actor's behaviour as heroic (in Techniques of Film Editing, Focal Press, New York 1953).*

I would argue that editing is also a crucial creative act in written composition, and I have included some rudimentary work on photographs in the book in order to make a link between photography, film and writing.

Key

☺ = individual work

☺☺ = pair work

☺☺☺ = group work

Plan it!

Introduction

Planning has to be used with judgement. There is no point in insisting on a plan for *every* piece of writing: some kinds of writing, like argument essays, benefit from being carefully planned, whereas others, like stories, are often planned in the head and/or evolve as they are written. Similarly, writing that depends heavily on its reception by an audience may need to be planned (as well as drafted and edited), whereas off-the-cuff communications do not warrant such careful preparation. The nature of an assignment should determine whether you will need a plan, and what kind of plan you will need.

Aims

This unit aims to provide a basic planning sequence, from initial and unorganised notes to a well-structured plan. Its function is partly to demonstrate, but also to offer a model which students may wish to try out and incorporate into their practice.

Methodology

The unit is arranged in clear stages. It is important to let the students choose their subject, and the initial listing of aggravating things is a way to effect this (as well as being an important stage in the planning and composing process). It would be helpful to have large sheets of paper for this unit – one way to operate is to complete the whole unit on one sheet, so that the process is visible. Pens of different colours help to distinguish the drafted from the editorial marks.

What next?

This seminal unit stands on its own, and could be followed by any of the other units in the book. It can be returned to from time to time.

Possible extensions

This could form part of a larger project on planning, either within English or across the curriculum. Comparisons are possible with plans of buildings, with early sketches in art, with hypothesis forming in science, and with design projects in CDT.

And, of course, the plan composed in this unit by each of the students can form the basis of a substantial piece of written work. Once the plan is complete, it would be frustrating not to go on to write the composition itself.

Looking at Instructions

Introduction

There is a balance in this book between informative/descriptive/referential writing, persuasive writing and expressive writing. This is the first unit in the **informative** mode.

Aims

To compose accurate instructions, and to be able to carry them out.

Methodology

It is essential that the instructions written by the students are carried out, in order to test their accuracy and appropriateness. This will make for an active lesson, and you will have to make preparations regarding materials and use of space in the school.

What next?

See Unit 3, *Follow that Guide!* (Informative writing 2).

Possible extensions

Although the 'tasks' used as examples in this unit are fairly immediate (tying shoelaces, etc.), it is possible to apply this approach to activities like the composing of rules for a club or (fictional) organisation. This might well tie in with a novel or play that is being read by the class. Then, taking the idea one step further, students could write instructions for surviving school or some such ordeal – in ironic vein.

Follow that Guide!

Introduction

This unit should follow Unit 2, *Looking at Instructions* (Informative writing 1), but not necessarily in the same week. The piece of work resulting from this unit should be substantial enough for a coursework folder and/or for use by other members of the class.

Aims

To develop awareness of sequence in the writing of instructions, and to make the writer sensitive to the needs of the audience.

Methodology

Students should be given time to select their subject, and can be encouraged to think of *presentation* as well as content: the manual could take the form of a booklet or pamphlet.

What next?

See Unit 10, *Giving directions* (Informative writing 3).

Possible extensions

Arrange for the students to see some official material that purports to inform or instruct: brochures, manuals, fire regulations and drills, etc. They could rewrite or revise some of these, and better still, visit the institutions which produce the materials, interviewing the staff responsible for their production. Such visits, of course, would require pre-planning and the co-operation of the establishments and staff concerned. A critical review of such material is a further possibility.

A poet's-eye view

Introduction

Poetry is an ideal form in which to draft and edit, for at least two reasons. First, poems are usually shorter than most other texts, so it is possible to reconceive the whole more easily than is the case with prose. Second, the conventional emphasis on the importance of individual words in a poem means that sharp focussing is necessary – and revising may well be a way of achieving this.

Aims

This first unit on poetry is largely for demonstration purposes, showing the stages through which a young writer has gone in order to produce a poem.

Methodology

Rather that starting with a given subject and a list of words on the board, as seems to be the practice in some schools, let the students choose their own subject to observe closely. They might want to use magnifying glasses or microscopes; they might want to observe for homework or outside school. The sequence from then on is clear; detailed notes (possibly in list form); writing each observation out as a line; rearranging the order; adjusting the vocabulary; writing a final draft.

What next?

See Unit 7, *Poetry choice* (Poems 2).

Possible extensions

Displays of the process of writing the poems, from early observations to the final pieces.

Collecting the poems from all the students into a book, with an introduction, contents, etc.

5

<table>
<tr><td>**Format**
Written ☺</td><td>**Duration**
About 1 hour</td></tr>
</table>

A Tiny Problem

Introduction
This lighthearted unit provides an introduction to the practice of **editing**.

Aims
Reading text critically with a view to editing it down (i.e. reducing the length) and thereby making its meaning clearer.

Methodology
Students will need a pencil or pen of a colour other than black to make their marks on the given letter. As it stands, there are 330 words: could the letter be reduced to say 200, then 100, then 20 words? The new versions should be written out, and then the students can compose a similar letter of their own.

What next?
See Unit 11, *Putting it in a nutshell* (Mini-sagas).

Possible extensions
Although personal letters are one of the forms of writing that seem least in need of drafting, there are occasions when drafting such a letter might be a good idea (occasions when exact wording and sequencing is important). Can your students think of such occasions?

6

<table>
<tr><td>**Format**
Written and oral ☺</td><td>**Duration**
About 2 hours</td></tr>
</table>

Once upon a time. . .

Introduction
This unit uses photographs to generate **narrative writing**, exploring the connection between narrative in film and narrative in written form.

Aims
To alert students to the importance of sequencing in narrative, and to enable them to try out various sequences on the way to composing a story.

Methodology
First, have the students cut out the photographs. They may put them in any order, and will gain much from trying out various sequences (there is quite a number of possible sequences – mathematicians might like to find out how many!). A plan will probably not be felt necessary: students will want to go straight into a first draft of the story.

The fascination of hearing each other's stories will be greater, due to their common source.

What next?
See Unit 12, It all began . . . (Narrative 2).

Possible extensions
Students can cut pictures from magazines, making their own bank of images for use in activities such as this one. The pictures can accompany the written stories as illustrations.

7

<table>
<tr><td>**Format** ☺☺ &
Oral and written ☺☺☺</td><td>**Duration**
About 1½ hours</td></tr>
</table>

Poetry choice

Introduction
This is an activity designed to generate talk about the **quality of poems**, and it could follow on from Unit 4, *A poet's-eye view* (Poems 1).

Aims

To encourage discussion and decision-making in small groups; to promote consideration of the quality of poems, based on criteria that will emerge during the discussions; to teach techniques of reporting back; to give the opportunity for the (collaborative) writing of a short report.

Methodology

The students work in groups of three or four. Give out sets of the poems, and ask the students to read through *all* of them first. Then, within each group, one person reads one of the poems and discussion can begin as to the good and bad points of each. From here on, it is best to leave each group to come to a decision in its own way, as long as you remind the students that they have to justify their decision to the rest of the class.

Limiting the report to 100–150 words uses skills of compression, but if pupils find it too restrictive, the report could be between 400 and 500 words in length.

What next?

See Unit 14, *A first class poem?* (Poems 3).

Possible extensions

A school poetry competition.

Format	☺☺☺	Duration
Oral and written	☺	About 1½ hours

8

Picture it!

Introduction

There is an editorial element in the choosing of subjects for photographs and in the way the photographer 'frames' his or her shot, but the first editing stage (after the selecting from the contact sheets) is that of **choosing the best shots for particular purposes and audiences.**

Aims

This unit gives practice in selection and the application of judgement; it also highlights the notion of different audiences. The connection with editing in writing is implicit, and there are writing assignments to follow the work on the photographs.

Methodology

The photographs should be cut out by the students, who can work in small groups for the first part of this assignment. Small-group discussion can move to whole-class debate before the individual work on captions and articles.

What next

This unit could be related to Unit 7, *Poetry choice* (Poems 2), and/or could lead on from Unit 6, *Once upon a time. . .* (Narrative 1) to Unit 12, *It all began. . .* (Narrative 2).

Possible extensions

Some students could shoot a roll of film and go through the editorial process on their own material. This works best if there is a purpose in mind for the photographs, like the illustration of a manual (see Unit 3, *Follow that Guide!*) or choosing a series of photos for use in a photo-story.

Format	☺☺☺	Duration About 1
Oral and written	☺☺	week of lesson time

9

Pen-friends?

Introduction

This unit focusses on the writing of a script *for performance*, and assumes that the script will be written **collaboratively.**

Aims

To produce a short play-script collaboratively. This will involve decision-making, discussion, drafting, editing and rehearsal, with a view to further revision of the script before its eventual performance – live or on tape.

Methodology

This is described quite fully in the unit itself, but some further points may be of help:

- Groups should be carefully constituted to ensure that the individual members work well together.
- It may help to assign roles within the group: director, scribe, editor.
- On the other hand, students often like to *write* in role, and keep their own copies of the script as it evolves.
- Guidance should be given as to length; and a time limit set for the project as a whole, so that the students know they are working to a particular deadline.

What next?

Further collaborative assignments such as Unit 43, *Hold the front page!*

Possible extensions

If this approach works well (and one of the most important outcomes of this assignment will be the talk that is generated), collaborations can take place in story writing and even novel writing. (See *Collaboration and Writing*, ed. Morag Styles, Open University Press, 1989.)

Format	Duration	
Oral and written ☺☺	About 1 hour	 **10**

Giving directions

Introduction

The importance of precision in **giving directions** is paramount. This assignment builds on earlier units concerned with **informative writing,** but also involves speech.

Aims

To encourage precision in giving instructions.

Methodology

This assignment works best in pairs, and each student should have a copy of the map.

What next?

This unit can precede or follow the other units on informative writing, or be combined with them in the same lesson.

Possible extensions

There is the opportunity here for developing encounters between people – involving giving and receiving directions – in role-play and drama. Confusing and/or humorous situations can be explored. *The Highway Code* could be rewritten to confuse the public rather than enlighten them.

Format	Duration	
Written ☺	About 1 hour	 **11**

Putting it in a nutshell

Introduction

In the late eighties, *The Sunday Telegraph Magazine* and BBC Radio 4 ran competitions to see who could write the best '**mini-saga**' of fifty words. Setting a tight word limit for a narrative forces the writer to draw on editorial skills in order to meet the requirements of the form. As you will see from the examples printed, as well as if you look at the collections published (*The Book of Mini-Sagas I* and *II*, Alan Sutton Publishing), the term 'saga' is used loosely:

what emerges in most cases is a poem, not always in narrative mode.

Aims

To compose a statement in fifty words, thereby drawing on editorial skills in order to meet the requirements of the form.

Methodology

Encourage free drafting first on whichever subjects

the students wish to write. These drafts should then be edited down (or more rarely, up) to the fifty-word requirement. This can be done on a competitive basis in the classroom, or in the school as a whole; also the mini-sagas produced can be collected in a publication or in displays.

What next?

Counting the length of texts leads naturally on to writing reports of specific lengths for newspapers, or to summary. See Unit 25, *Headline news* (Report 1); and Unit 26, *The bare facts* (Summary).

Possible extensions

The fifty-word limit is an arbitrary one, of course. Experiments can take place with shorter or longer 'sagas', and with different forms. Most of the mini-sagas in the collections are set out as poems, but this need not be the case. It would be interesting to take a single mini-saga and set it out in a variety of ways, judging the differences between them.

Format	Duration	
Oral and written ☺/☺☺	2 hours plus	 **12**

It all began. . .

Introduction

This unit extends the work attempted in Unit 6, *Once upon a time. . .* (Narrative 1) where only four photographs were offered; and in Unit 8, *Picture it!* (Looking at photographs), where there was also the possibility of using four photographs in a similar way.

Aims

To alert the students to the effect of different structures and sequences of the same material; and to make connections between image and word.

Methodology

As there are over 40,000 different possible combinations of these photographs, it is highly unlikely that two children in the same class will come up with the same sequence; and even if they do, it is unlikely that their stories will be the same. This unit can either be attempted individually, or students could combine into pairs and thus introduce an element of 'talk' to the assignment.

If some students cannot manage to include all eight images in a constructed story, they can work with any number they like.

What next?

This unit is likely to produce substantial writing, but could be prefaced or followed by other units on story writing, Unit 27, *Story-time* (From storytelling to story writing); and Unit 28, *Behind the scenes* (From story to script).

Possible extensions

As suggested in Unit 6, students (and teachers) could collect images for use in similar activities, and then use these images to illustrate narrative, descriptive and persuasive writing. The basic principle at work here is akin to that behind the composition of film and TV productions, and explorations into film-making and film-study may be possible.

Format	Duration	
Written ☺	At least 1½ hours	 **13**

Going places

Introduction

It is easy to collect spare brochures from travel agents (as well as details on houses from estate agents), and they can provide excellent raw material for revisions and rewriting.

Aims

To focus on **persuasive writing** with a view to making new texts from old; concentration on synonyms and antonyms, and on the particular style of **travel brochures.**

Methodology

In preparation for this activity students can be asked to go to travel agents to collect brochures that are no longer current, either prefacing their visits with letters or calling in unannounced. This in itself is useful practice in persuasive talk and writing. Once the brochures have been acquired, either cut out suitable passages and pages and hand them to the students, or give each student a brochure and ask each of them to select a page to rewrite.

Dictionaries of synonyms and antonyms may be useful.

What next?

This kind of writing is halfway between informative and persuasive, so this unit can be linked to units concerned with those aspects of writing.

Possible extensions

The writing of an entire holiday brochure, complete with photographs cut from magazines and other brochures. This can produce highly entertaining and very specific work in English. Again, role-play and drama can be based on the completed brochures, e.g. a family complaining about the quality of a holiday (both in writing and orally).

Format	Duration
Written and oral ☺ ☺ ☺	About 1 hour

A first class poem?

Introduction

This unit can be in a series of lessons on **poetry** (see Units 4 and 7) and enables the composition of a poem by a group and by the class as a whole. The modest initial demand of a line from each student on a particular theme is built upon, and the resultant collaborative talk will address many issues in poetry and poetics.

Aims

To promote consideration of the 'line' in poetry; to generate talk that will enable decisions to be made, and will focus on the nature and technique of writing poetry; to concentrate on a particular theme.

Methodology

This is fairly explicit in the unit itself. It will help if the groups (fours or fives) sit around tables, so that

they can both write and discuss. The size of each group should be adequate to produce a stanza, and the poem as a whole may be made up of as many stanzas as you have groups in the class (6 or 7?). You, as co-ordinator of the event, may well need to put some finishing touches to the poem towards the end of the lesson – or you can assign this job to someone in the class. The poem can then by typed up and displayed – perhaps as a large-scale illustrated poster.

What next?

See Unit 15, *Paper-chase poem* (Poems 4).

Possible extensions

This activity can be conducted on a group basis as well as on a whole-class basis. The advantage of trying it with the whole class first is that the process is demonstrated to all, before groups, and then individuals, try it for themselves.

Format	Duration
Oral and written ☺ ☺ ☺	45 minutes plus

Paper-chase poem

Introduction

This unit is another example of how a **group can edit disjointed material.**

Aims

To encourage talk about the sequence and shape of a poem.

Methodology

Students will need scissors and paste for this assignment, and they work in groups. There is no right answer here, although the cut-up lines are from this completed poem, which was composed by a class of 8 to 9 year olds.

Cats

Cats slip like water through your hands
with legs that stretch like rubber bands,
ears that point all around
and paws that patter on the ground.

They're playful, silly, sleek and slow
with eyes like pearls, all aglow.
They crawl up fences, jump in tubs;
they're friendly little tiger cubs.

These baby tigers on the run
have fluffy hair that climbs in sun.
But underneath, you'll hear some say,
they're hunters on the search for prey.

Jaguars, panthers, lynxes, lions:
nothing safe you can rely on.
They're cheetahs that can sit in trees
or acrobats on a trapeze.

Jumping down from high-up places.
They leave no dirty muddy traces
even when they've been in rain.
Their noses rub on the window panes.

Little terrors in your house,
nightmare-bringers to bird and mouse.
Fluffy balls of feline fur:
listen to those kittens purr!

Note: Experience suggests that providing the 'right' answer after a sequencing exercise often undermines the progress made in deciding on a shape for the poem. The original poem is given here for your information and for use at your discretion.

What next?

In a reversal of the usual procedure, the teacher can act as composer of a poem, using single lines supplied by each of the students in the class. An overhead projector will be helpful here, so that the whole class can see the successive drafts and comment accordingly.

The earlier units on poetry demonstrated ways into composing poems that should be accessible to most students, and this unit covers very preliminary techniques for shaping language into poetic form. The next step would be to use poetry workshop books suitable for years 7–9, like Sandy Brownjohn's *Does It Have to Rhyme?* (Hodder and Stoughton), Ted Hughes' *Poetry in the Making* (Faber and Faber), Jill Pirrie's *On Common Ground* (Hodder and Stoughton), or my own *Into Poetry* (Ward Lock Educational) and *Poetry* (Macmillan English Modules). For years 10–11, try Richard Andrews and Ian Bentley, *Poetry Horizons I & II* (Unwin Hyman).

Possible extensions

As well as moving towards work on a more individual basis, there is still scope for choral and group work in poetry. See the books referred to above.

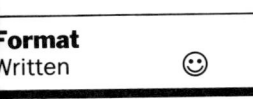

| **Format** Written ☺ | **Duration** About 1 hour | | **16** |

Have you read . . .?

Introduction

Publishers' **blurbs** are useful (short) forms for practice in class because they are connected with the students' reading, involve the skills of summarising and using persuasive language, and can be a part of the network of recommendations about books. Another feature of blurb writing is that the plot of the work described must *not* be given away: a blurb is an invitation to read, not a full summary of the text it refers to.

Aims

To compose a short text that strikes a balance between giving information and persuading the reader to pick up the book referred to and read it. To generate interest in reading, and to work through drafts until the finished piece is word-perfect.

Methodology

It is important in this assignment that the students choose their own books to recommend to each other (and possibly to a wider audience within and beyond the school). A word limit (and target) may be set to add an edge to the drafting and editing process.

What next?

Blurbs are a useful preliminary to the writing of reviews, in-role writing and other work to come out of the reading of literature; but they needn't be confined to fictional texts. It would be well worth writing a series of blurbs on a range of different kinds of books (manuals, plays, encyclopedias, pamphlets, etc.).

Possible extensions

A range of blurbs can be culled from various books for purposes of comparison. The titles of the books could be matched with the blurbs by the students.

17

Format		Duration
Written	☺	1 to 1½ hours

Have a closer look

Introduction

This is another unit which uses photography as a means to understanding an editing technique in writing.

Aims

Through drafting and rewriting, to focus on **detail in description**.

Methodology

Cut the photocopied pages in half and distribute the wider-angled shot first. Encourage the students to create a character from this picture. They can work in the present tense in descriptive mode (e.g. "This is Sue. Sue Fairbrother. She . . ."); or in the past, narrative mode (e.g. "It was Christmas Eve, and Angela Fortune was thinking of the past year. Little did she know . . . ").

When the character has been sufficiently established, the second photograph can be distributed. Ask the students to provide a more detailed description of the features, and for their suggestions about the character and her way of life. This additional writing can either be added to or spliced into the existing draft.

What next?

See Unit 18, *Action time!* (Focussing on detail 2) and other units on photography and writing.

Possible extensions

The work on character completed so far in this unit can form the basis of a full-scale short story. An interesting question to ask (of a crucially editorial nature!) is where will the description of the character go in the story as a whole. There is no need for it to come first, just because it has been written first.

18

Format		Duration
Written	☺	About 1 hour

Action time!

Introduction

This is a fairly self-explanatory unit, borrowing techniques from film.

Aims

To **focus on detail** by 'slowing down' the description of an 'event' or moment, breaking it into its constituent parts; the expansion of texts.

Methodology

Although this activity works best if the writing is set out in poetic form (line by line), it is equally possible to write in prose, doubling the number of words each time a new 'take' is made (see below). Students should go as far as they are able in this activity: some will manage eight lines (or, say, a sentence of eight words), whereas others will want to push this piece of writing as far as they can.

What next?

See further work on the relationship of film and photography to writing in Unit 36, *A very strange case* (Solving a mystery).

Possible extensions

The prose version of this assignment, mentioned above, can be worked on like this: instead of building the text line by line, students could start with a single-word sentence (e.g. "Morning.") The next sentence would have two words in it, the one after that four, and so on (e.g. "Morning. I wake. The sun creeps in. It crawls over the window sill, then falls . . .").

| Format ☺ ☺☺ ☺☺☺ Oral | Duration About 1 hour | **19** |

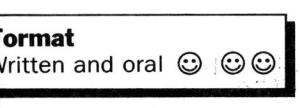

Here is the News

Introduction
This unit concerns itself largely with the **sequencing of material for television news broadcasts.**

Aims
To provoke thought and discussion about the relative importance of different items of reportage; to encourage experimentation in sequencing.

Methodology
This (and other sequencing activities) works best if the items of news are cut up before work on them begins. Physically moving the pieces of paper around on the table enables even the weakest of students to come to decisions and to see the emergent text they are creating. Once decisions have been made by the pairs or groups, a spokesperson from each group can report back to the rest of the class, justifying the order – and further argument may ensue.

What next?
Other work on news, e.g. Units 20 to 23 (Sub-editing 1 to 4); Units 25, 29, 30 and 38 (Report 1 to 4).

Possible extensions
The completed news scripts can be performed by students, preferably in pairs (*News at Ten* style), and can provide a model for their own news scripts. These could concentrate on particular kinds of news, like sport, school news, humorous news, etc. Outside reports can be built into this model (as well as advertisements at the half-way stage!). This work, in turn, can lead on to an analysis of broadcast news.

| Format ☺ ☺ ☺☺ Written and oral | Duration 45 minutes to 1 hour | **20** |

Rough stuff

Introduction
Newspaper sub-editors work 'in-house' (i.e. they work at desks, and don't go out reporting) on the details of the reports and features that will appear in the paper. Unlike editors, whose job is largely to decide what goes in the paper and where, the sub-editors handle the text that comes in from the reporters (by phone, by fax, by computer, by telex, handwritten or roughly typed on paper) and prepare it for printing.

This unit is one of a series on newspapers.

Aims
To teach some editing and proof-reading skills; summarising through writing headlines.

Methodology
The next three units (and others later on in the book) deal with particular aspects of in-house editing. This unit provides less confident students with an opportunity to adopt an editorial 'approach' and to practise basic editorial skills. The errors are deliberately simple, to build up students' confidence before they attempt to cope with more complex errors related to sense and structure.

Students can tackle either one or both of these roughly typed reports, in pairs or singly. The advantage of pair work in this instance is that discussion will take place as to the accuracy of the text.

What next?
See Unit 25, *Headline news* (Report 1) and/or Unit 26, *The bare facts* (Summary).

Possible extensions

Texts can be created with deliberate mistakes in them for sub-editing and proof-reading by others in the class. In the production of newspapers, journals and magazines within school, sub-editing becomes a natural and necessary part of the process of reaching the final product.

21–23

Format	Duration
Written ☺	45 minutes for each one

Focus on spelling, Focus on sentence structure, and Short and sweet!

Introduction

Each of these units will require a single lesson and a homework, or the best part of a double lesson, though the intensity of the concentration needed suggests that a single lesson is the maximum time one should devote to such an assignment at one sitting.

Aims

Each unit aims to focus attention on *one* particular aspect of writing: the first on **typographical and spelling** errors, the second on **paragraphing, sentence structure and punctuation,** and the third on **verbosity.**

Methodology

The approach should be fairly self-evident in each of these assignments, but your judgment will decide whether to ask students to rewrite the passages or simply to mark them – as an editor would.

What next?

See Unit 39, *Dotting the 'i's* (Putting it right), which combines a range of different types of errors in the same passage.

Possible extensions

Exercises like these are fruitless unless they are tailored to the needs of individual students in your classes – or groups of students. But there is considerable scope for discussion between students as to how to correct the errors; and in structural and stylistic matters there is often more than one way of expressing an idea or feeling, and talk about the variant possibilities will be both interesting and useful. Students might like to prepare texts for each other to work on.

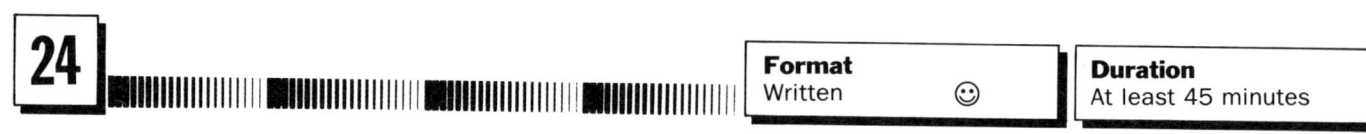

24

Format	Duration
Written ☺	At least 45 minutes

Putting your ideas in order

Introduction

The **ordering of material in an argument** is always open to question, and, as students often find it hard to construct arguments, this assignment gives practice in decision-making about the sequence of points.

Aims

To encourage the consideration of the arrangement of points in an argument; to try alternative sequences, and to judge the best one for a particular purpose.

Methodology

As in the other assignments which involve sequencing, it pays to cut up the various sections for the students.

What next?

The sequence of points in any piece of writing is important, whether it be a narrative, description or argument. It would be well worth considering this with the students from time to time, in relation to the composition of different kinds of writing.

Possible extensions

The writing of an argument essay. These tend to be best if the student is allowed to choose his or her own subject and title and feels strongly about the issue.

Headline news

Introduction
This assignment is a revised version of an original written by John Noble of *The Observer*.

Aims
To encourage selection of relevant material; ordering of the material; summarising; drafting; working to a deadline and to a word limit.

Methodology
This unit is fairly explicit. Students should equip themselves with pens of colours other than black so that they can make editorial marks on the photocopied sheets. They are looking for the key details to make up a story, and will have to sift the essential from the less important. The time deadline makes the activity more authentic, though judgement must be used in this respect.

What next?
See further units on reporting.

Possible extensions
Many of the units in this book provide models for students to apply to the particular contexts and events of their own lives. In this case, the collecting of information in notes and the movement through selection, drafting and editing to a final report can serve as a model for their own investigative reporting.

The bare facts

Introduction
This unit is similar to Unit 25, *Headline news* (Report 1), except that in this case the original text is an existing report rather than notes.

Aims
As for the work in Unit 25 (Report 1), students should take an editorial pen or pencil to this article and work through it, deleting sentences and paragraphs that are less important than others. Finished versions can be compared in groups, and then by the class as a whole.

Note: The opening paragraph that has been omitted from the article reads as follows. *A millionaire and former gold-bullion dealer fled naked from an upstairs window after stabbing an intruder in his Westerham home in the early hours of last Friday morning.*

What next?
This is the first of a series of units on report writing. See also units 29, 30 and 38 (Report 2, 3 and 4).

Possible extensions
Students could supply a new headline for their abbreviated story. They may also wish to work on further articles and reports cut from newspapers.

Story-time

Introduction
This is one of several units in the book devoted to the relationship between speech and writing. This first unit focusses on the **telling of stories** and on a comparison between a told story and a written version of the same story. Such comparison draws attention to grammatical and structural questions, as well as issues of length, the inclusion of description, and so on.

Aims

To encourage the telling of anecdotes, tales and stories, all of which presuppose or display an ordering of experience in the mind; transcription of recordings and resultant reflection on the nature of spoken stories. Then to encourage the production of good written versions of the same stories, and careful comparison of the two versions: spoken and written.

Methodology

This activity works best if you have laid the ground beforehand. The very least that is required is some time for the students to reflect on, discover and rehearse the stories they are going to tell in class.

For Part 1, students can be grouped in threes or fours, each group (ideally) equipped with a cassette recorder and assigned to a quiet space in the school where they will be uninterrupted (you will have to book these spaces before the lesson). The students should be asked to return to the lesson at a certain time, having decided which is the best story of those told. They should be prepared to play that story back to the class as a whole, or (better) present a retelling of that story.

The next step is to transcribe at least one story from each tape. This is time-consuming, and is best carried out by one student from each group – prefer-

ably someone with typing or wordprocessing facilities. These transcriptions can be brought back into class and serve as a basis for Part 2.

The methodology for Part 2 is fairly evident from the unit itself. Students can be asked not only to discuss the differences between the two texts, but also to list them for purposes of discussion with other groups or in the class as a whole.

What next

Textual analysis of literary writing like this leads on to the next unit, *Behind the scenes* (From story to script) and to units about style.

Possible extensions

There is enormous scope here for making a taped anthology of 'told' stories, especially if the school has facilities for editing audio tape (either from recorder to recorder or by cutting and splicing). Another possibility is to record and transcribe stories told by people in the community.

Motivation will be greatest when the student is working on his or her own material. A collection of short stories written by the class and based on original tellings of those stories (particularly if the tapes and/or transcripts are kept) will make a fascinating publication for the class or school library.

28

Format	☺☺	Duration
Oral and written	☺☺☺	1 week of lesson time

Behind the scenes

Introduction

'Genre transformation' involves a good number of editorial decisions, and in the case of a move **from story to script** the handling of dialogue and narration is crucial.

Aims

To translate a story into script, thereby asking the students to look closely at the story and to decide what to retain, what to leave out, and how to adjust other elements of the language to suit the new form.

Methodology

Again, the notes in the unit itself are explicit. Once the students have decided and agreed on the division

of the story into sections, these sections can be assigned to groups to start the work of adaptation. Some sections will be easier than others, and your judgement will be called upon to assign the sections appropriately.

What next?

This unit is self-contained, but links with others in the book that focus on literary texts.

Possible extensions

It is possible to try this approach with other short stories (and note that this story is particularly short), or indeed to adapt other genres to script or story.

Going National

Introduction

Reports from local newspapers have been used in this book because the scale of story is more akin to the lives of secondary school pupils than many of the stories in the national press. There is no reason, however, why national newspapers should not be used in the same way.

Aims

This is another assignment involving the **reduction of text** and therefore necessitating summary, re-writing and (in this case) **reframing for a different audience.**

Methodology

Some discussion of the different audiences of local and national newspapers will be helpful before the students attempt this assignment, and of the range of different stories in the two kinds of newspaper.

Supply or ask the students to bring in copies of *The Daily Mirror* and *The Independent* so that the students can study the style and tone of each paper and compare the two. They will need to think carefully about *where* in each paper each article might appear, and what headings to give their revised reports.

What next?

See the following unit, *Editorial changes* (Report 3).

Possible extensions

A reversal of the situation presented in this unit, with a rewrite of a story that originally appeared in a national newspaper for the students' own local paper, will involve the skills of expansion (it may be necessary to invent details). If it is possible to visit the offices of the local paper, or invite some of its editorial staff to talk at the school, the experience will be given an extra dimension.

Editorial changes

Introduction

This unit provides an example of a typewritten report for a local newspaper, and is part of a series of units on reporting.

Aims

To ask students to look closely at the changes made as a story progresses into print: changes in meaning, detail, grammar and punctuation.

Methodology

This unit involves not only the identifying of the changes made by the reporter but also the explanation of them. Students can work on their own to read the report and typescript, move into pairs to identify and discuss the changes, and then gather as a whole class to compare notes.

What next?

See Unit 38, *Time for order* (Report 4).

Possible extensions

As in the first unit on reporting (Unit 25, *Headline news*, Report 1), students may wish to trace the evolution of reports from early notes of observations, through drafts, to typescripts and the printed version. Collaboration with local newspapers will make this study more interesting, and displays showing the whole process can be mounted in school. The very appearance of such a display in school will make students more aware of their own writing processes, and about language production in general.

Format		Duration
Written and oral ☺ ☺☺☺		1 to 1½ hours

Getting into print

Introduction
The scope for **travel writing** in English is tremendous, and far exceeds the clichéd 'What we did on our holidays' idea. See the suggested extension work for directions in which this kind of writing can be taken.

Aims
To put the student in the role of editor of a narrative, informative text; this will involve decision-making about paragraphing, style and clarity of expression.

Methodology
Cut the photocopied sheet into two and let the students grapple first with the unedited text. When they have written their edited version of this, the second (published) text can be introduced, thus provoking discussion in groups and then in the class as a whole.

What next?
See the following unit, *A matter of style!* (Style 1).

Possible extensions
The text in this unit was used as an introduction to a guide book on Mexico, and as such is not typical of most travel writing, which tends to tell the story of a journey and/or describe a place. Let your students try an extended piece of travel writing: one which may be built up over a few days, and which conveys a distinct impression of either a familiar local journey or an unusual journey that might be made during a weekend or school holiday.

Format		Duration
Written ☺		About 2 hours

A matter of style!

Introduction
This unit marks the beginning of a section of units which look at language rather more closely than previously.

Aims
To draw attention to the variety of **styles** possible in the writing (and rewriting) of a simple story, and, by giving students practice in writing in some of these styles, to extend their language repertoire. The given examples, though eccentric, are manageable and fun; they make their point through excess of style.

Methodology
Having read the basically notated story and the version told as an official letter, students should choose freely from the list of possible styles and be encouraged to make up more of their own.

What next?
There are various 'styles' and forms included in this book (e.g. informal letter, report, brochure, poem). Students could refer back to some of the work already completed.

Possible extensions
Queneau's book is published by Marion Boyars and is well worth acquiring for amusement and for the department library. As well as each student trying three or four styles (and thus having enough material for an assignment to be included in a coursework folder), everyone in the class could try to write the same story in a different style. The results could be collected in a small book, as well as read out and/or displayed.

Format		Duration
Oral and written	☺☺ ☺☺☺	At least 1 hour

Tell me about it

Introduction

This is one of the few units in this book that is directly concerned with a spoken form (though almost all the units involve speech as part of the work).

Aims

To encourage **interviewing** in role, and then to foster a critical awareness of the nature of spoken text through a transcription of the interview.

Methodology

There are two ways of recording the interviews: on tape (followed by a transcription) or in note form during the interview itself. In the latter case, you need two interviewers: one to ask the questions and respond to the interviewee, and the other to make notes. Comparison of experience between those that work together in writing up an interview from notes on the one hand, and those who transcribe on the other, will make for an interesting discussion in itself.

What next?

See Unit 34, *Meeting point* (Interviews 2).

Possible extensions

Before the real interview is undertaken in the next unit, it is worth discussing interviewing technique. In particular, are the questions best prepared beforehand or asked spontaneously? Is there an order in which questions should be asked? Should personal questions come in early or late? How can the interview be brought to a proper close?

Format		Duration
Oral and written	☺	About 1 week

Meeting point

Introduction

This unit follows on from the preparatory work in Unit 33, *Tell me about it* (Interviews 1).

Aims

To conduct an interview with a member of the public; to transcribe the interview and use it as the basis for an article about that person; and therefore to develop skills of communication in public, of comparing spoken and written forms, and of selecting material and reframing it for 'publication' in writing.

Methodology

Much of this is explained in the unit itself. How far you, as teacher, take this work, is a matter for you and the students to decide.

What next?

Students may like to compose a guide as to how to interview, once they have gained the experience of the second interview. On the other hand, 'How *not* to interview' may be more amusing.

Possible extensions

Connections with people outside the school, or with others teachers and non-teaching staff within the school, extend the horizons of the classroom and may well suggest further opportunities for work of this sort. Inviting a visitor to the English class, for example, is something the students could organise: it involves letter writing, making arrangements to suit both parties, meeting the guest, laying on tea, deciding how the session will run, and so on.

Format		Duration
Written	☺ /☺☺	1 hour plus

Think about your readers

Introduction

One of the most successful activities for 13 to 14 year olds in recent years has been composing texts for children in primary schools. These are often stories, written and illustrated in the secondary school and then given to and/or performed in the primary school. This unit focusses on a different kind of writing.

Aims

To **rewrite a transactional text for a particular audience;** simplifying and finding the appropriate tone.

Methodology

Students should be encouraged to take a pencil or pen to the given text, selecting material they will use in their rewritten versions.

What next?

As with many of these later assignments, the logical next step is to move from the school into the world outside; to move from a simulated assignment to a real one. And this could turn out to be a real assignment if you know any younger children who would benefit from a guide like this. Make sure the students really get to know the needs of the audience before they start writing.

Possible extensions

As well as a real guide for young people, other assignments of this kind which suggest themselves are: a tourist guide to the area, a local's guide to the area, a transport guide, etc.

36

Format		Duration
Written and oral	☺ ☺☺ ☺☺☺	At least 2 hours

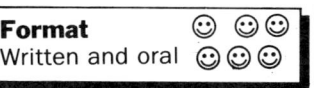

A very strange case

Introduction

This unit puts to use some of the drafting and editing skills learnt in other units. It is a simulation, of course (as all work from a book of texts like this must be), but is a step closer to the kind of problems solved in the 'real' world with the help of notes, drafts and editing.

Aims

By supplying evidence, to provide the beginnings of an exploration-cum-problem-solving exercise for students to solve in pairs or small groups, drawing on skills such as note-making, drafting, editing and decision-making, and on imaginative speculation.

Methodology

Distribute the first sheet, allowing 15 to 20 minutes for discussion and note-making, and the rest of the lesson for the first draft write-up of the incident in whichever form the students wish to use. The second sheet should be introduced when the first draft is 'finished'. Simulated interviews of witnesses can take place at this stage, before a revision of the original writing in the light of this new evidence.

What next?

Although there are no further examples of this kind of unit in the book, it provides a model for students to create their own collections of 'evidence' to form the basis of a similar project.

Possible extensions

Apart from the suggestion in the previous paragraph, there is scope here for a trial (as mentioned in the unit itself); for writing in the role of the figure in the photographs (or other people involved in the incident); for script; and for drama based on what came before and what came after this incident.

37

Format		Duration
Written	☺	Abour 1½ hours

Selling off the page

Introduction

This is another typical 'real world' assignment, based on an actual visit to a company which wanted to rewrite its **promotion brochure.**

Aims

To select from and adapt source material in order to fashion an informative and persuasive text; practise in defining a suitable sequence for information.

Methodology

The approach is determined by the nature of the material, though students will find coloured pens helpful for the initial selection or highlighting of information.

What next?

See Unit 40, *The art of selling* (Brochure 3).

Possible extensions

Try making contact with a company that will let you have plenty of their promotional material, rewrite it and send it back for comments. Many companies will be happy to co-operate if you explain the nature of your project in full.

Format		Duration	**38**
Written	☺	About 2 hours	

Time for order

Introduction

This unit provides further experience of working with reports, except that the element of time is introduced as a factor influencing the arrangement of data.

Aims

To encourage flexibility in the arrangement of reports; to generate discussion about structure; to attempt the writing on a report which moves backwards and forwards in time.

Methodology

Cut up the eight paragraphs of the initial report to make the job of experimenting with arrangement that much easier.

What next?

See other units related to work on newspapers.

Possible extensions

Cut stories, reports and articles from newspapers and then cut them up into paragraphs to analyse the time sequence underpinning the text. You could also analyse and report on the varying and average lengths of paragraphs in different newspapers, as well as in newspapers as compared to other (e.g. literary) forms.

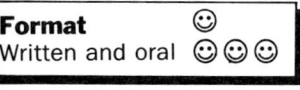

Format		Duration	**39**
Written and oral	☺ ☺☺☺	1 hour	

Dotting the 'i's

Introduction

Earlier units, which broke down errors into types, were necessarily rather contrived. This unit presents a more realistic piece of unedited text for students to apply their editorial skills.

Aims

For students to cast an editorial eye on a text, and then compare notes on suggestions for structural, lexical, orthographic, typographic and stylistic changes.

Methodology

Twenty minutes of individual work followed by group and class discussion is probably the best approach here. Then see below.

What next?

Students should be encouraged to apply this editorial approach to their own, as well as to others', writing.

Possible extensions

To continue the story.

The art of selling

Introduction

This unit takes the earlier work on writing brochures a stage further.

Aims

To set the writing of brief informative and persuasive texts in a 'real' context.

Methodology

Students can either start by designing the layout of the brochure or by writing the text (and subsequently tailoring it to suit purpose and format).

What next?

As this is a fairly sophisticated assignment, the next step would be to take this kind of writing beyond the confines of the school, into political and/or marketing fields.

Possible extensions

There is no reason why quality work of this nature and in this format cannot be included in coursework folders for assessment, perhaps combined with other similar 'short texts'. Or, of course, the work can be of greater length.

Who was Ben Hall?

Introduction

Recognising **bias** in language is an important skill. In this unit, two deliberately biased accounts of the same man are set side by side so that students can compare them and then write an *unbiased* account from the evidence presented.

Aims

The recognition of bias in written texts; the selection of factual information and rephrasing of it for a particular purpose.

Methodology

It is possible to cut off the preliminary explanatory material and simply present the two passages. Which one depicts Ben Hall as hero, and which as villain? The unbiased passage can be shortened to whatever length you think appropriate, thus introducing condensing as well as selection.

What next?/Possible extensions

Take neutral accounts of events in newspapers and add bias to them.

Ways of working

Introduction and aims

A unit is included here to instigate discussion and debate in the class about **wordprocessing** and its bearing on drafting, editing and other aspects of the act of writing.

Methodology

Because the students will have varying degrees of experience in wordprocessing (including no experience), this unit is to be used with judgement. Much use of wordprocessing is uncritical of the constraints which wordprocessing imposes upon the act of writing, but it is important to be aware of these as well as of the liberating effects. Give this unit to students who do have at least some experience of wordprocessing, and use it as a springboard to debate and/or to the writing of manuals to help those in the class who are at various early stages of development in wordprocessing.

What next?/Possible extensions

A network of wordprocessing training can be set up within the class/school so that those students with expertise can help those without. This is an area where some students may have a good deal more experience than some of the teachers.

| Format  Oral and written | Duration About 1 week |  | **43** |

Hold the front page!

Introduction

This assignment involves design as well as decision-making.

Aims

To employ both large and small-scale editorial skills; to select illustrative material and write captions; to make decisions in small groups; to write headlines; to draft, discuss and complete news stories, and other material.

Methodology

Large (at least A3, but preferably A2) sheets of paper will be best for this assignment.

What next?/Possible extensions

To produce a newspaper for an audience outside school is a massive but worthwhile undertaking. The same principles of composition apply, but on a larger scale; and issues of duplicating costing and distribution have to be addressed.

MAKING PLANS

Plan it!

First, make a list of things that make you angry. These can be anything from irritating little things, like the habits certain people have in your family, to much larger issues, like the way schools are organised, the lack of facilities for teenagers in your area or the fact that some children in the world are hungry.

Example:
sexist jokes
too much work
useless television programmes
big-heads
people with short tempers
being told off
pollution
racist people

Try and get at least six items on your list.
Compare notes with a partner.

Now look again at your list. Put a ring around the topic that makes you most angry. Cover a page with your thoughts and feelings about this topic. Why does it make you feel angry? Give details and examples. Do you think everyone feels this way about this topic? Don't worry, at this stage, about the order in which you put things down.

Next, draw lines or boxes around points that go together, like this, until you've covered all the points you put down. Then number them in the order you think they might go best in your essay.

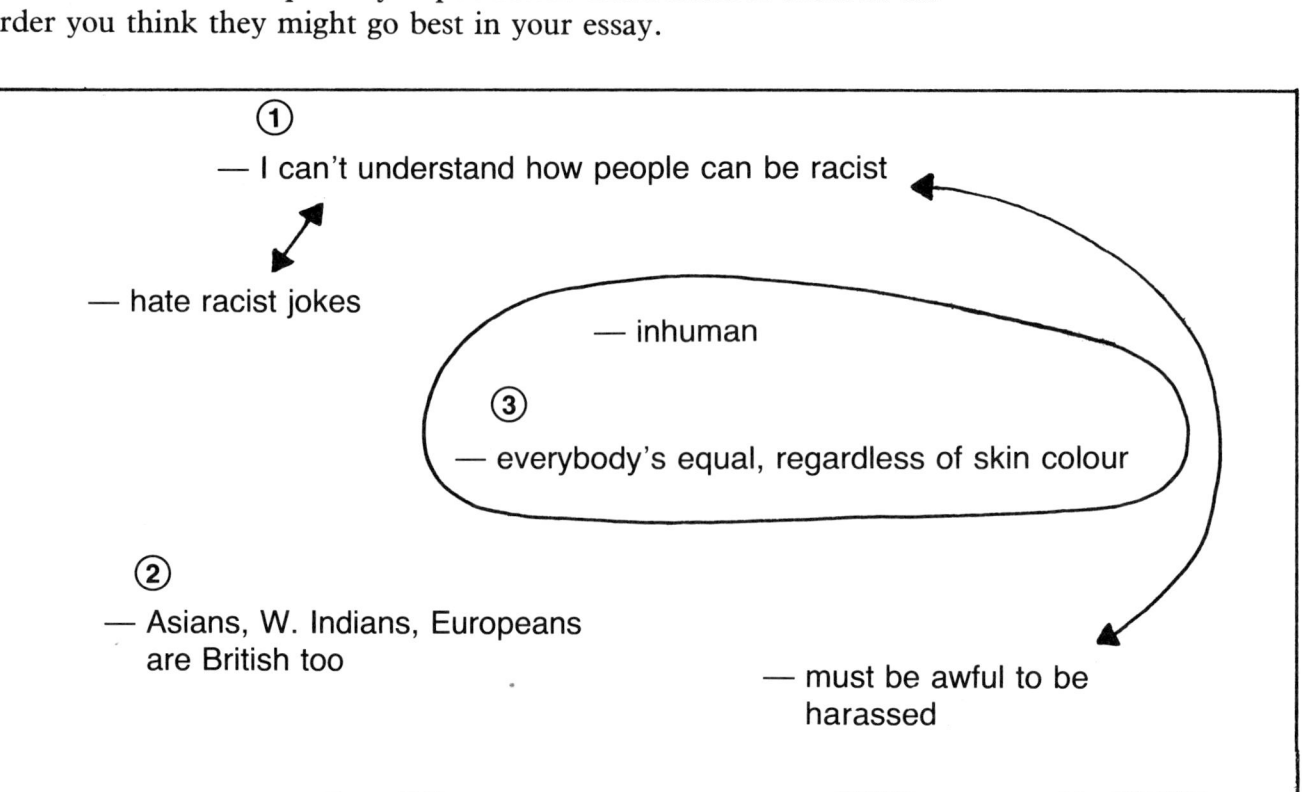

Write out the points again, this time in the order that you intend to use them. Perhaps each idea that you boxed or circled will make up one paragraph in your essay; perhaps you will need to add more material or more ideas to one section; perhaps you can combine two points in one paragraph.

This stage of the planning should tell you where the gaps are in your piece, and where you need to research more or think more. You might have a lot of work to do here before you go on to the next stage . . .

① • I can't understand how people can be racist.
   — I hate racist jokes
   — must be awful to be harassed

② • Asians, W. Indians, Europeans might be British too.
   — immigration has dwindled. Many people from ethnic minorities were <u>born</u> here.

③ • It's inhuman to be racist.
   — everybody's equal

④ • Racists must be insecure. What is their problem?

When you feel you have enough material to make your case convincing, check again to make sure you have got the sections in the right order. With the example above, would it have been better – or just as good – to have the sections in a different order? For example: ③ ① ④ ②

Try this with your own notes.
If you like, cut them into sections and try them in various sequences.

Use this planning technique whenever you think you need it.

Looking at
INSTRUCTIONS

Writing instructions is not as easy as you may think.

Try to write clear instructions, *without diagrams*, for:
- tying shoelaces
- finding a particular room in school
- tying a tie

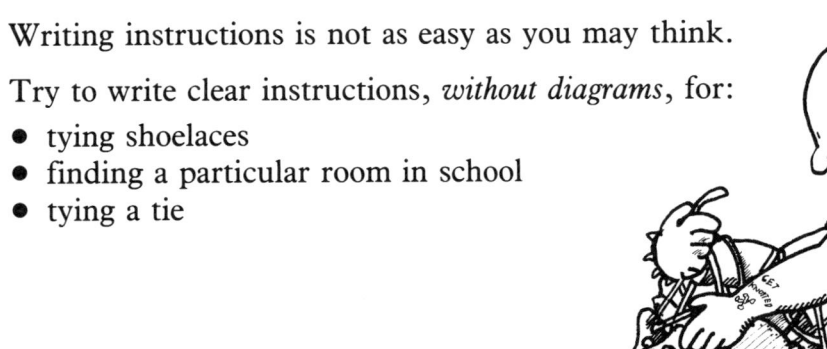

Test your instructions by asking someone else to follow them as though they are carrying out each activity *for the first time*.

Make revisions to your instructions as you go along, where you find that they are not clear enough for the person following them, or where you have left something out.

When you have finished the set of instructions, try them again to make sure they work.

Experiment with the sequences and format until you find the best version.

Follow that Guide!

Write a brief manual which will help and guide readers in making or playing something. For example:

- a recipe
- a game (like *Scrabble* or *Cluedo*)
- a model
- how to use a computer

Here is an example from a set of guidelines and instructions to give you an idea of the kind of writing you need to produce.

How to give the kiss of life

In an emergency, if someone has stopped breathing, give the kiss of life immediately. You should continue until there is normal breathing or until help arrives.

1 Place victim on his or her back. Clear anything blocking the mouth.
2 Pull the head back and lift up the chin.
3 Pinch nostrils together (except in the case of a child).
4 Cover his or her mouth with your own (but for a child, cover the mouth and nostrils).
5 Blow gently into the mouth, checking that the chest rises.
6 If the chest does not rise, pull the head further back and try again.
7 Remove your mouth and wait until the chest falls.
8 Blow again, and repeat every five seconds until the person breathes normally or medical help arrives.

An essential feature of this activity is that you actually try out your instructions when you think you have the first draft completed, so that you can revise and improve it where necessary.

A poet's-eye view

One way to work toward a sharp and powerful piece of poetic writing is to start very 'small' and gradually work up to poetic form. In this example of work from a first-year pupil in a school near Doncaster, the poem had its beginnings in detailed observation and a simple listing of words to describe the object of observation – an owl.

fragile	Sharply	gentle
Soft	Swiftly	feathery
Wingly	Swooping	huge
brightly eyed	Rounded	huckly claws
Smothly	Spungly	knife like beak

This list was edited by the pupil so that she could focus on some of the words, and add others. A second draft was written, with a line being devoted to each of the words selected from the initial list.

The fragle feathers their like a coat,
The Soft big body which belongs to him,
There's also evil eyes look at it's pray,
Sharply of the beak it is,
How Swiftly he flys in the Sky,
The swooping of the wings looking for his pray,
The gentle of the pray he picks up,
His huckly claws stick in and hold on,
The Beak pushes in and pulls out the meat,
Then Smothly he flys again off
He goes up, off into the Sky,
The feathery wings don,t make a sound but beat,
The huge body gets darker as it goes into the
      distance.

A poet's-eye view

Here are two later versions of the same piece. With a coloured pen, mark any changes that you can see were made as the poem evolved. Compare notes with a partner to see if you have both spotted the same changes.

The owl and his pray

* The fragile feathers their like a coat,
The soft big coat which belongs to him.
There's also evil eyes look at it pray.
How swiftly he fly's in the Sky ?
The swooping of the wings looking for his pray
    which he finds.
* The gentle of the pray he picks,
His huckly claws stick in and hold on,
The Beak pushes in and pulls out the meat,
Then Smoothly he flys again off he goes up
    off into the Sky.
The feathery wings don,t even make a sound
    but beat
The huge body gets darker as it gets into the
    distance,
* And can not see it any more.

The owl and his prey.

I was sat in a tree soundless,
day dreaming,
When I saw him,
And I couldn't stop whispering.
The fragile feathers are like a coat,
The soft big coat which belongs to him,
Also evil eyes looking at its prey.
How swiftly he flies in the sky.
The swooping of the wings staring for his prey
    which he finds.
He picks up his prey and soft,
His hulky claws stick in and hold on.
The beak pushes in and pulls out the meat,
Then smoothly he flies again,
Off he goes, up off into the sky.
The feathery wings don't even make a sound,
But beat to silent music of the fields.
The huge body gets darker
As it goes into the distance.
The field was neglected and alone,
But I had Seen an owl for once,
And I had to go home.

Now use this same technique of working from first-hand observations to build up your own poem or prose description of a person, place or creature.

A Tiny Problem

A friend of yours is going away for the weekend and wants you to help him write a letter to someone, asking her to look after a rather unusual pet while he is away. Here is what your friend has written so far: it's rather long-winded. Can you rewrite it so that it reads more clearly? You can change the layout too if you like.

24 High Rise
Chimeley
Cheshire

Dear Patti,

I've got this thing to ask you and I don't quite know how to put it, but anyway here goes. You see, I've got this pet, and I'm going away for the weekend with my parents to Liverpool for a holiday. We don't need a holiday but Mum and Dad thought we did, and so we're staying in a beach chalet in sunny Merseyside. The point is that Tiny will be left all alone with no one to feed, wash or take him for walkies. You're probably doing something else – and why not? You've got your own life to sort out – but I wondered if you could look after Tiny for me. I promise I'll pay you back one day, by looking after your plants or taking your grandma for a walk or whatever.

Tiny likes to be fed six times a day, and you'll find his food if you take a spear into the forest behind our house and go and kill it yourself. He eats anything from other pets – like dogs, hamsters and pussies – to deer. You'll also need to wash his hands before and after meals and sweep up the kitchen because he leaves it in a bit of a mess, to say the least.

Then there's bath time. He likes you to scrub his back and his belly with iron wool, and lather his ears in washing-up liquid. Whatever you do, don't shampoo his hair because he hates that and will probably attack you. He has to be dried with Mum's hair dryer and it takes about an hour.

You can take him for a walk in the park after dark, but don't let him off the leash, otherwise he will hit the headlines in the morning paper (like the time when he went off with the lollipop man).

Thanks very much for offering to do this. I hope I'll see you when I come back.

Yours,

Carlton

P.S. I forgot to mention: Tiny is a lion.

> You might like to compose letters of your own about pets more incredible than a lion!

Once upon a time...

Cut out the photographs so that you can arrange them in different sequences.

Put them in an order that suggests a story to you. You will have to create names for characters, define settings, and imagine the action taking place between as well as in the photos.

Your story can take place – as can any story – over a short period of time or over many years. And, as in any good story, everything must fit together.

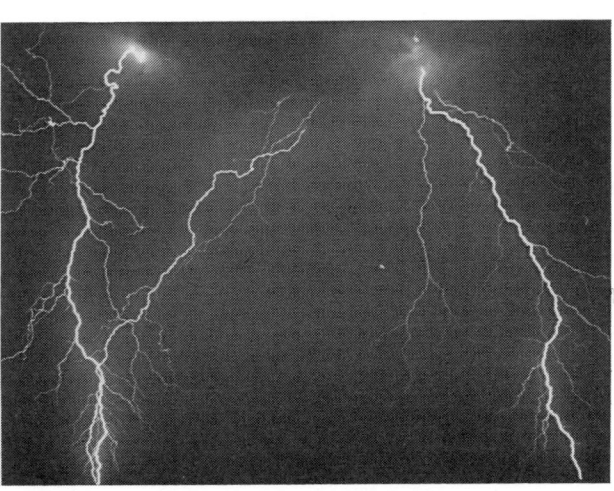

When you have finished the story and read it to others in the class, ask yourself whether you could have changed the sequence of photos and still written the same story.

POEMS 2

Poetry choice

You have decided to compile a poetry anthology for readers in your year at school, and you have room for three more poems. In groups of three or four, decide which of the following five poems you will include – and be prepared to justify your decision to the rest of the class.

The Tiger

In the jungles of night,
There is not a twitching of leaves.
For amongst the trees,
There is a tiger with eyes bright burning.

Those flaming furnaces of fire
Pierce the phantom forest.
He stands fearlessly and clasps his prey
With his claws.
Merciless against death.

The tiger stands majestically in the moonbeams
His symmetrical attire glistening with the stars.
He starts
The scent of blood
The colour red
Entices him.
He tortures his prey till dead.
The trees shudder and shake.
At the sound of his footsteps the animals quake.

Yet with his pride
And princely stride
This beast
As he feasts
Has to set his dreams aside.

Hemlata Joshi

The Dedicated Teacher

Clasping the bars, her face contorted in pain,
she cried 'Is there a spare child?
A child I can buy, borrow, anything?
I'll give you a dollar or even two,
I need a child.
They've tried animals, birds and old men
but I need a child.
Don't you understand, I need to teach.
I can't eat or sleep or do anything.
Give me a child, I'll raise it to three dollars.
Is anybody there?
I need to teach a child,
I'll teach it everything I know
but give me a child, or I'll die.'

Tessa McInnerny

Sheep Fair

The auctioneer stands dripping,
wringing out his beard into a puddle at his muddy feet.
The sheep huddle sadly together,
trying to stay out of the rain,
like Saturday shoppers in a sudden shower.
Their wool soaks up the rain like dirty white sponges.
They smell of wet sweaters on washing day.
The farmers' hats fill up and spill and spill again.

Victoria Burgess

Poetry choice

Midnight

Tick, tock, tick, tock,
Seconds to go till twelve o'clock.
Now the start of the terrifying chime
Like a continuous haunting rhyme.
Hark, the dogs begin to howl
And hear the scary hoot of the owl.
The windows begin to rattle,
   the floorboards begin to creak
And people are startled out of their sleep
To hear the horrifying screech of the bats
And the devilish hiss of the bloodthirsty cats
And far away a hideous laugh
As the night disappears into the past.
Then one o'clock strikes and all is peace
And all these strange happenings cease.

Hugo de Burgh

The Reality

Listen;
We all want to live,
Like a big happy family,
We all want to live,
In a quiet, peaceful land.

So why are people
Putting money and power
Before love?
So why are people
Making war movies
And calling love stories
Old and boring?

We go to health clubs and wealth clubs,
We go on skin treatments,
To get rid of a few wrinkles
When thousands of faces are fading away.

Listen;
We all want to live,
Like a big happy family
We all want to live,
In a quiet, peaceful land.
So, why don't we just DO that?

Julia Kim

When you have decided which three poems you will include, write a brief report, giving the reasons for your decision. Work on this report in pairs and make it 100–150 words long.

How are you going to arrange your report? In a list? As a narrative account of how you came to the decision? In some other way? Discuss this first in pairs before you start the actual writing. And when you do start, are you both going to write a version of the report and check each other's or will you work on one version together?

Now consider the following editorial points:
- *If you had to reduce your choice to just **two poems**, which poem would you omit and why?*
- *If, in the end, you could only include **one poem**, which one would it be?*
- *Choose one of the five poems and make up three questions about it that you would like answered.*
- *Are there any 'difficult' words in any of the poems that you would want to explain for your readers?*
- *Would any of these poems benefit from illustration?*

LOOKING AT PHOTOGRAPHS

Picture it!

Here are three different photographs of the same street market. Each one could be used to illustrate a different sort of article about street markets, for example, a story in the local paper about how the market gives good value for money for the local community.

Choose one photograph and write an article which you think the picture would illustrate well.

Pen-friends?

Writing something in pairs or small groups is not easy, but people often do it in business, in theatres or in other contexts. Try collaborating in the writing of a short play for performance in class or recording on tape (a radio play).

First, decide how many are going to work together in the writing and performing of this play (two or three is probably the best number; four is about the maximum).

Then decide what your play is going to be about, or which incident or story you want to start from. You might want to focus on an issue of current news interest.

Next, decide how many scenes you are going to have. One idea is to have the same number of scenes as there are people in your group, so that you can write a scene each.

That brings us on to the next, and very important question: if you are going to collaborate, how are you going to share the work? Here are a few ideas for you:

1 As suggested above, each of you could write one scene, once you have decided what the plot is going to be and who the characters are. When the first version of a scene is finished, you will obviously want to read it aloud together and see if it fits alongside the other scenes written by the group.

2 Another approach is to sit around a table, with one of you acting as scribe as the others compose the play together. You can either each speak in role as the character you intend to play, or work together to compose the dialogue as you go along.

3 If you use the second approach, there will come a point when it gets difficult to work together, e.g. when you need to work at home or have several copies of the script to read. Then you will have to make photocopies of your draft script, or copy it out; and write longer speeches individually and splice them into the text at particular points.

4 Once your script is in shape you will need to try it out to see if it works. Do this several times, stopping afterwards to discuss what changes you want to make to improve it. These may be small changes, like altering a word here and there, or reading in a different tone or at a different pace; or they might be larger changes, like switching the order of scenes, writing new scenes, changing who says what, etc.

Giving directions

Here is a map of part of a town in England.

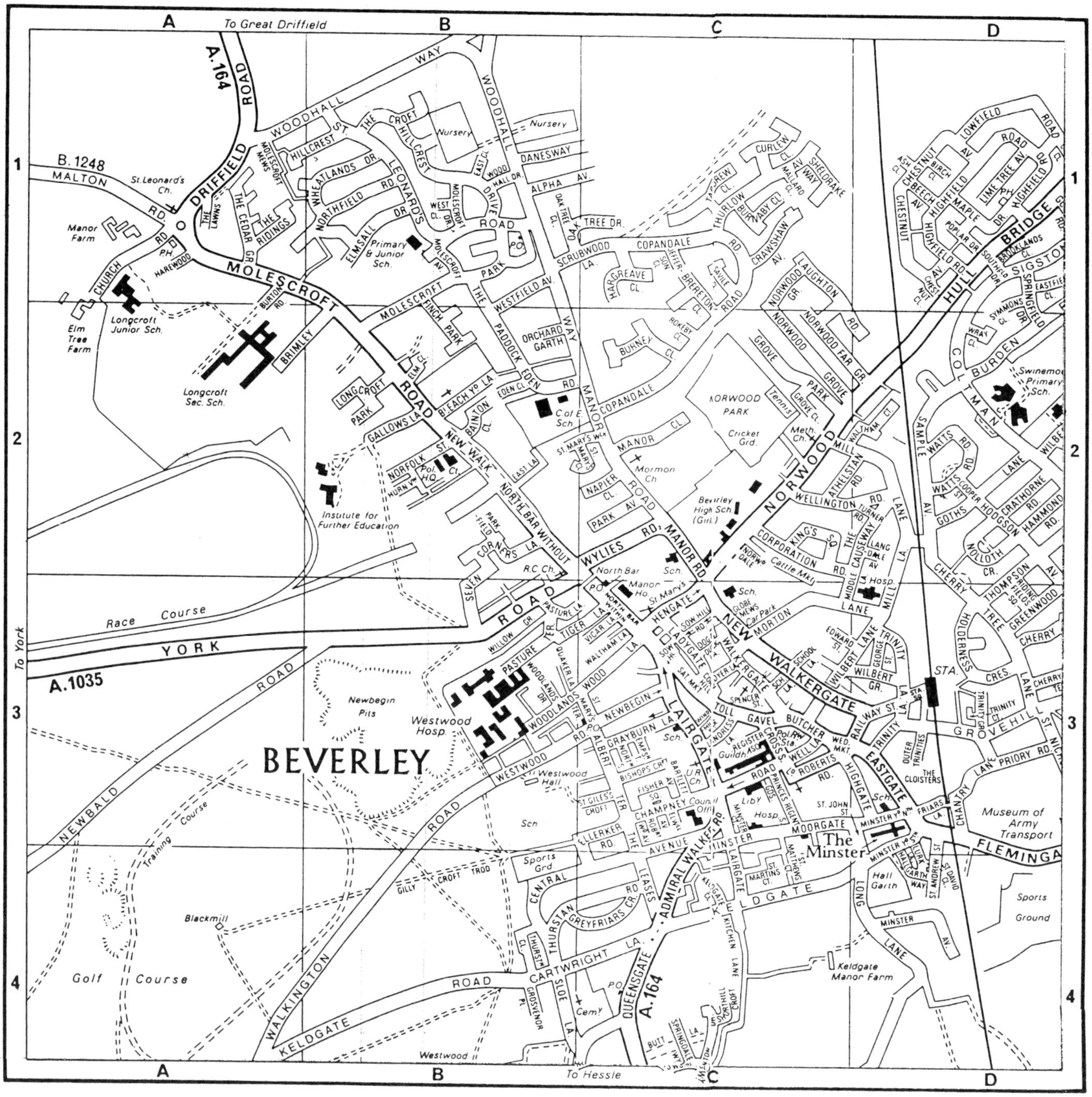

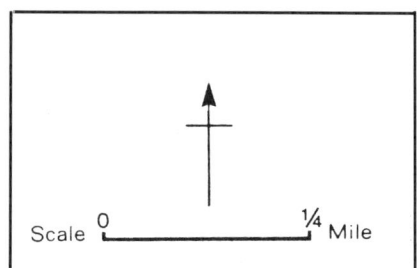

Work in pairs. **A** chooses a point on the map and gives **oral** directions to **B** as to how to get from there to an unnamed place. Is **B** at the right place in the end?

Reverse roles so that **B** gives **A** directions for another journey.

Now try the same exercise, but in **writing**. Both of you write out your directions and then try them on each other. The directions must be revised as necessary in the light of the trial.

Scale 0 ———— ¼ Mile

Putting it in a nutshell

Here are two examples of mini-sagas (which isn't a very accurate name, as *saga* is an Old Norse word for a long tale of the legends of Scandinavia). Nevertheless, these 50-word texts are fun to write. The best pack a great deal into their fifty words, some even breaking into poetic form.

BACK AND FORTH

*A middle-aged
couple playing tennis,
parted at the net, not married,
not divorced but separated.
Although they leave,
the net remains between them
and their child bounces back
and forth like the ball
on the court.
They may be happier apart but
the ball has to absorb the
punishment.*

**Lisa Nixon
Age 12**

INVINCIBLE

*He will not live, they said.
He is now thirty-one.
He will not walk, they said.
He ran the London Marathon.
He will not be independent,
they said.
He owns a flat in town.
He'll be a loser all his life, they
said.
He beat them all,
hands down.*

**Jane Grinaway
Age 14**

Start by roughing out a short and very compressed story – don't worry at this stage about the quality of the story. Write it out as a prose draft. Count how many words you have so far.

Edit up – or, more likely – down to around fifty words. As you do the editing, consider what you are saying in the story. Are you satisfied with it, or does it need rethinking (in part or as a whole)?

As you get to the stage of polishing your story, check the number of words and decide how you want to set it out. It could be like the 'sagas' on this page, or in some other form. (Remember that ordinary prose is one option.)

NARRATIVE 2

It all began . . .

In an earlier assignment in this series, you were offered four photographs to arrange in a sequence that would tell a story; and then were asked to write the story. This time, there are eight photographs, and over 40,000 different sequences that you could arrange them in.

Eliminate one of the photographs, but try to use the other seven to write another story. This one might well be more complicated, and longer!

Before you write your story, write plans (not drafts) of at least *two* possible stories that you could construct from these photographs. Make these two initial plans very different, and compare notes with others in the class to see what they have created. If necessary, you can reduce the number of photographs you work with to less than seven.

You may, of course, cut out the photos so that you can arrange them more easily; and you may want to try several sequences before you come up with the one that will form the basis of your short story.

BROCHURE 1

Going places

Here is an excerpt from a travel brochure, inviting you to holiday in Gumbet, Turkey.

Gumbet beach

The Turkish flag might have been inspired by Gumbet: the long, crescent shaped beach with the diamond sharp stars that shine after the setting sun has dyed the sky red at the end of another perfect day.

Gumbet is perfect for kids of all ages; the ones seeking to master swimming, snorkelling, water-skiing, the jetski, boardsailing. . . and there are canoes and dinghies to hire. In fact, it might be the perfect watersport learning centre — especially in the mornings when wind and wave conditions are less challenging and there are fewer practised exponents to make one suffer the frustration of feeling inferior.

The beach is backed by many bars and lokantas, ranging from the simple featuring one Turk with a grin and a freezer full of beer and coke, to quite plush spreads with a good menu plus a nice thatched bar to sit in. The hotels and bars also hire out sun umbrellas and loungers, which provide a welcome haven after scampering up the hot sand from the sea.

Galloping inflation has caused a shortage in the lower denominations of banknotes, so if the vendor hasn't got the odd lira you need as change, he'll offer you anything from a cup of tea to a stamp as compensation.

If you're feeling too lazy to walk to a bar, locals parade up and down the beach with cold drinks, corn on the cob and even toffee apples.

If the mornings are for exercise and appetite building, the afternoons are assuredly for napping — though remember to have a trusted friend at hand to oil and turn you from time to time to avoid a spit roasting effect.

Sea, sand and sustenance are arranged in concentric curves around the bay overlooked by derelict windmill towers that might long ago have been crafted by some giant sand-castle builder.

And when, if, you have exhausted the attractions of Gumbet, Bodrum is but a good hike, short dolmus trip or affordable taxi ride away.

Alter the text to **put people off** going on holiday in this place. Some of the changes you will have to make may be quite subtle, and you may find a dictionary of synonyms and antonyms helpful.

Make sure your altered version reads as smoothly and convincingly as the version above. Read it out to others in the class, and make any final adjustments you feel necessary.

You can then work on individual pages from different brochures, and even produce your own brochure.

A first class poem?

For this game, everyone needs a small piece of paper and a pen. Glue and scissors will help, but are not essential. Work in groups of four or five.

Each person writes one line describing a childhood fear: it should be something personal to each writer, for example:

> *"Chickens pecking at me through the wire . . ."*

or

> *"Getting lost in high-street crowds, and seeing nothing but grown-ups' knees. . ."*

(Note that a line of poetry can be shorter or longer than a line of writing on the paper.)

Next, each group decides in which order their lines sound best. It may take some time to find a satisfying order, and one person in the group may need to add a few words to make the whole thing flow more smoothly. The lines can be written out again, or glued into place.

Then the completed stanza or verse (for that is what it is now becoming) is handed on to the teacher or a student who collates all the stanzas from the various groups. His or her job is to put the various stanzas in a satisfying order, and then to read the emerging poem to the class.

It may be that this last stage of composing needs more editorial work. Decisions will have to be made about the regularity (or otherwise) of the rhythm; the place of rhyme; the overall 'flow' of the piece.

Here is an example of one verse (your own verse need not rhyme!)

> *Chickens pecking at me through the wires,*
> *Getting squashed under tractor tyres;*
> *Getting lost in high-street crowds, and*
> *   seeing nothing but grown-ups' knees,*
> *Being stung by wasps and bees.*

Paper-chase poem

The lines of a poem called *Cats* have been jumbled up. Work in a group and see if you can put the lines back together in an order that satisfies you. Try out different ideas and talk about them, until you all agree on an order.

and paws that patter on the ground.

Cats slip like water through your hands

with legs that stretch like rubber bands,

Fluffy balls of feline fur:

They leave no dirty muddy traces

ears that point all around

even when they've been in rain:

They crawl up fences, jump in tubs;

they're hunters on the search for prey.

But underneath, you'll hear some say,

with eyes like pearls, all aglow.

have fluffy hair that climbs in sun

listen to those kittens purr!

Jumping down from high-up places.

nothing safe you can rely on.

Jaguars, panthers, lynxes, lions:

They're cheetahs that can sit in trees

Their noses rub on the window panes.

or acrobats on a trapeze.

These baby tigers on the run

Little terrors in your house,

they're friendly little tiger cubs.

nightmare-bringers to bird and mouse.

You will find that as the poem takes shape, you will have to decide whether to divide it into stanzas (verses) or not.

They're playful, silly, sleek and slow

Have you read . . .?

One of the editorial jobs in a publishing house that deals with fiction is the writing of blurbs to go on the back covers of paperback editions of novels and collections of stories.

Here is an example of a blurb from the Unwin Paperback edition of *Hunter's Moon* by Garry Kilworth.

Tonight, a hunter's moon shines down on Trinity Wood. It shines on Breaker, lead hound of the hunt, who lies dreaming of the fox-bones he will snap and crunch. It shines on O-ha the vixen, and on old Gar the badger. It shines on Sabre, the vicious ridgeback hound. He has a score to settle with a small red fox who once outwitted him – an insult he will never forget. And under the same moon, far away, Camio the American Red Fox, paces up and down his zoo cage, listening to the cries of a thousand fellow prisoners and dreams of freedom.

'the one talking-animal book you *must* read . . . a thrilling read'
DAVID V. BARRETT
in *White Dwarf*

'an enchanting tale'
Western Evening Herald

Write your own blurbs for books you have read. Here are some points to bear in mind:

1 *Remember that you are trying to persuade someone to read this book.*
2 *You mustn't give away the whole story, but you might want to select part of it to entice the reader.*
3 *You might like to include your own quotations from reviews, as the Unwin Paperback blurb does in the example above.*
4 *You need to make sure that the finished blurb is word-perfect, and about the same length as the one above.*

FOCUSSING ON DETAIL 1

Have a closer look

Look at the woman in the first picutre and begin your description. Then from the more detailed photograph, you should be able to develop this character portrait more fully.

Action time!

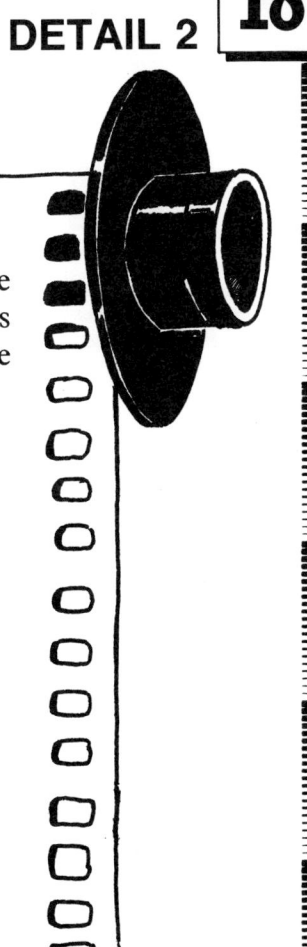

When film moves into slow motion, you sometimes see detail much more clearly – for example, a bullet passing through a piece of wood, or athletes in a race crossing the tape. You can try this technique in writing by 'slowing down' the description of a simple action, like this:

First, write down a simple action in one line:

> *I met her at the corner of the street.*

Now make that two lines, without expanding much on the action that took place:

> *In my new jeans and T-shirt,*
> *I met her at the corner of the street.*

Double this to make four lines, still keeping to the same subject:

> *At four in the afternoon,*
> *with my heart pounding, and*
> *in my new jeans and T-shirt,*
> *I met her at the corner of the street.*

Double it again:

> *At four in the afternoon*
> *after a long hot day in school,*
> *as if I were building up to a big exam*
> *and with my heart pounding*
> *in my chest like a puppy freed from its chains;*
> *in new jeans and T-shirt*
> *and a pair of old tennis shoes,*
> *I met her at the corner of the street.*

Could you do it again? And then go to 32, 64, 128 lines?!

> *At four in the afternoon,*
> *after a long hot day in school*
> *in which nothing went right –*
> *I was in trouble with the Head*
> *when I got into a fight –*
> *as if I were building up to a big exam*
> *and with my heart pounding in my chest,*
> *like a puppy freed from its chains*
> *or a horse without reins;*
> *in new jeans and T-shirt*
> *and a pair of old tennis shoes*
> *I borrowed from my brother,*
> *I stood waiting on the pavement*
> *thinking she was late*
> *and I'd have to go home without her — then*
> *I met her at the corner of the street.*

TELEVISION NEWS

Here is the NEWS

*Suppose the following news items formed the main news on TV one night. On your own, or in small groups, decide in which **order** you think the items should appear. Remember that news programmes usually start with the most important story and move down in order of priority, ending with a lighter story.*

The Minister for Sport, Thomas Nooligan, announced last night that he was recommending that all sportspeople should carry identification cards at all sporting events, and that spectators would now no longer be allowed to watch any sports 'live'. In future, they would have to enjoy the sports on their television sets.

Flossie, a six-month-old kitten, was found last night half-way up a chimney at her home in Esher, Surrey. Her parents, Mr and Mrs Felix of Catford Road, Esher, said they were relieved to find her again as she had been missing for several days. They had heard cries coming from above the fireplace but thought that it was the wind blowing down the chimney. Flossie's first act on being freed was to try and get back up the chimney.

The legal age for drinking alcohol in pubs is to come down to sixteen, after the Licensed Victualler's Association reported that young people act more sensibly if allowed certain privileges like this. It is expected that the recent trend in drunkenness among the 16-18 age group will decrease with the new drinking laws, and if the experiment is a success, the minimum drinking age may well be reduced to 12 in the next session of Parliament.

Fights broke out last night at the annual meeting of the Society of Vole Fanciers when it was announced that ferrets as well as voles were to be included in the title of the organisation. One campaigner for the Vole Protection League said that she was appalled that other committee members were considering an alliance with ferret fanciers. It could mean the end of voles in this country.

Thirteen-year-old schoolgirl Dawn Bray-King chained herself to the railings of her school yesterday in protest at what she claimed to be the refusal of the school tuck-shop to sell fruit instead of sweets to the pupils. Dawn is reported as saying that she was spearheading a campaign for healthier eating, and that this was the only way to draw attention to the issue.

Javelin star Sandy Templeton returned home last night from her triumphant performance in the European Games, where she threw a career-best 96 m. This beats her previous British record of 94·6 m. She said to reporters at the airport that she was tired and would be taking a holiday in order to recuperate.

Rough stuff

Here are two newspaper reports, in their original form as written by reporters. Obviously, some changes will have to be made in content, paragraphing, accuracy and presentation before the reports are published in a paper. Write out your edited versions, and give a headline to each report.

In the shock surprise of the 3rd round of the FA Cup yesterday, lowly Telchester Town beat Swanpool Athletic 2–0 in a breathtaking match at their tiny Butt Road ground in front of a capacity crowd of 16,500. Only ten minutaes after the staRT AND Telchseter were ahead with a headed goas from their ace striker MItch Blakely, who nodded in from a cross by returned hero John Sampson. Telchsetsre soaked up waves of Swanpool pressure, with Chambers, Jimson and McPhail all going close. Twice Swonpool hit the baR, and once the post. But manager Jock Tannadice's half-time talk obviously worked wonders on the East Angtlian team as they came out to score another through veteran ampaigner Dave Mistlewick in the 65th minute.
Swanpool couyldn't force hjome a goal despite all their pressure, anbd returned to Pearson Park to concentrate on the league. Telchsetr meet Rotherdale in the next round.

Teengae superstar Tanya Brown is opff to the StaTESnext week m to mstart her first North Ameri8casn tour. The success of her recent album 'Mersey Flights' won her a place in the hearts of Americans and she expexcts a sell-out in every city. The tour begins at the Shea Stadium in New York, venue for the big Beatels concert in the sixties, and nthyen she moves on to Wasjkhington, Baltimore, Phuiladelphia and Boston, before heading over to the West Coast for gigs in San Francisco and Los Angeles.
Asked about her plans for after the tour, she said "I'm not making any plans at this point. I think this could be the end of my career, it'll be so exzhuasting. Maybe I'll try something else after this."

SUB-EDITING 2

Focus on
SPELLING

These two pieces arrived on the sub-editor's desk one afternoon. They clearly need proof-reading. Can you play the role of the sub-editor, and make sure these are correct before they go to press?

There was a madjor oilspil late last night ten miles of the coast of Humberside, when two oil tankers colided, shedding there cargo of 1500 tons of crood oil into the North Sea.

It happened at 11.35pm, when the tanker Grease Princess appeered to move channells and head straight for the Copenhagen-registered Norland, which was at the time at ancher and waiting for cleerance to enter the port of Hull.

The Marine Rescue Service said that a full-scale allert had been put into action, and that police, fire and abulance servies were involved. So far, there have been reprts that sixteen (16) of the crew of the Norland were injoored, none of them serously. They have been taken to Hull general Hospital and will be dissmissed later today.

Another newspspaer for teengaers was lornched today in London, by Argosy Newspapers. It is called The Good News and aims, as its tytle suggests, to spred good news about acheivements of young people across the world, rather than convey the bad things some young people do.

It is internacional in flavor, including stories from as far afield as Nicaragua ('Young heroes of the frontline') and Hong Kong (a story about school children haleping in a transit camp for Vietnamese refujees).

This brings the total of newspapers for young adults to four. The Good news aims to include sports news, fashen, feetures about young people, an agony column, horrorscopes, crosswords and various competisions in order to attractas wide an ordience as possible. It costs 45p and comes out every Friday.

Give a title to each story.

Focus on SENTENCE STRUCTURE

Sentence structure and punctuation are often difficult to get right. Gaining confidence in this area means developing a good ear for writing that is read (or 'heard aloud' in the head), and being able to spot errors when they occur in your own writing. As a sub-editor, it is unlikely that you would come across a passage quite like the following one, but rewrite as much of it as you can so that it makes clearer sense. There is more than one way of getting it right!

Just sitting here makes me wonder if I will ever get out I mean only yesterday they gave me a note from the Governor which said they would be considering my case at the next review meeting well we all know that's in about three months' time in the meantime I have to sit in here and fester thoughts go astray I find myself dreaming of freedom probably to you that doesn't mean much but to me it means everything the freedom to walk down a street unchained simply to look in windows never intending to buy anything the freedom to talk to friends phone up my mum and dad to eat what I fancy and to drink whenever I please not least when I am thirsty all these little freedoms you miss when you're inside of course I also dream about meeting someone and setting up a home and perhaps even having kids it's not too late for that about going on holiday to Italy or the Caribbean about gardening in a little patch at the back of a house nothing grand just a few square feet to call my own space instead here I am stuck in a concrete cell eating food that's pushed in on a plate three times a day left alone with my thoughts

---

You might want to break it into paragraphs too!

SUB-EDITING 4

Short and sweet!

Sometimes language gets too flowery and longwinded, and we all wish for a straightforward voice to clear the air and make some sense. It is as if the speaker has decorated the window of language with paints, when all we want is to look through the plain transparent glass to grasp the meaning of what is being said.

Here is an overdone thank-you letter. Without reducing it to terseness by making it too short, see if you can rewrite it so that its style is clearer and more elegant.

Dearest Auntie Joanne,

I was delighted and very pleased to receive your present yesterday, and I don't really know where to start in thanking you. You are the kindest, most thoughtful aunt imaginable, and it really was nice of you to think about me so personally. In fact, the tissue-box holder was just what I wanted. How did you guess? Probably a little bird told you (in the shape of Mum), but however you found out it really was an inspired gift. Now I won't have to look at those unsightly tissue boxes, but instead can take a tissue (when I need one) from your elegant box. Thank you again.

Actually, not only is it the perfect size for the tissues that I buy, but it also matches the wallpaper in the bathroom. How did you do it?

I think I'll go and fill it now with a box of tissues. Thank you for thinking of me again this year.

Your loving niece,

Tiffany

You may also want to attempt a satirical version of this letter, by exaggerating some of the points.

Putting your ideas in order

Here are several paragraphs from an essay written to argue for the provision of dog toilets in a small town. The order in which they appear here is not necessarily the order in which they should appear. So cut up the sheet and arrange the paragraphs as you think best. Provide at least one alternative arrangement.

One of the most worrying things about finding dog mess on pavements and in parks, on grass verges and elsewhere in town is that children who love to play in these places are in danger of catching diseases from coming into contact with it. It is possible to contract quite serious diseases in this way.

Fines for fouling the pavement or the street seem not to have much effect. How many times have you seen anyone approach a dog-owner and threaten to report them to the police for breaking the law, even though the signs announcing the potential fines are displayed right there on the lamppost or wall?

There seem to be only two solutions. The first is for the council to provide dog toilets, hidden from general view, where dog-owners will be obliged to take their dogs. These could be financed by an extra fee being slapped on top of dog-licence fees, because no doubt they will have to be serviced and cleaned on a regular and frequent basis. The second is for each dog-owner to be obliged to clean up after their dog, as is the case in New York where you see dog-lovers clutching their 'poop-scoopers' as they take 'Rex' or 'Flossie' for walkies. I don't know which of these two solutions I would prefer.

The alternative is to tighten up on the law and practice as it now stands, with police spending more of their time on the lookout for offending dogs, and arresting them and their owners where necessary. Or perhaps we could strengthen the arm of the ordinary person and encourage a system of 'citizens' arrests'. As the tide of feeling moves increasingly against dogs and their foul habits – just as it has against smoking in public – this approach might work.

Only the other day I was walking on a patch of common land with my two-year-old sister and five-year-old brother, and we came home with dog mess on our shoes and – more worryingly – on my sister's hands and clothes. Why can't dogs, like cats, be more civilized about the way they go to the toilet?

One of the most distressing facts of everyday life in this town is that you have to watch where you're walking in case you happen to walk straight into some dog mess left on the pavement or in the park. This issue has been irritating me for some time, but now I find myself becoming increasingly angry at the number of times this has happened to me – and to my friends.

REPORT 1

Headline News

You are a reporter on The Freetown Gazette, *a local evening newspaper. You receive a phone call telling you there has been an accident on the motorway near your town, in which a plane has crashed into a bank at the side of the road. You go to the scene of the accident and this is what you see and do.*

1 The plane, a Boeing 737 airliner, is lying part on the motorway and part on the bank. Its nose-cone has broken off from the main fuselage. There is a good deal of chaos at the scene as rescue services attempt to get survivors from the wreckage as fast and as safely as they can.

2 Elsewhere on the road are the wrecks of five cars immediately affected by the crash of the plane, and several others have crashed into each other or veered off the road altogether. There is a tailback of traffic for several miles in both directions. Police are trying to divert traffic on to the A674 to bypass the scene of the accident.

3 There are 15 fire-engines, 12 police cars and 10 ambulances on the scene, with more arriving. A helicopter hovers overhead to ferry victims of the crash to the local hospitals, Freetown General and Keningsby County Hospital. TV crews and reporters from radio and other newspapers are also arriving at the scene.

4 You look at your watch. It is 4 p.m.

5 You speak to an eyewitness, Marilyn West, whom you record on your small tape-recorder. This is what she says: "I was walking with my boyfriend in the woods above the road when all of a sudden we heard this terrible noise, sounding like a big truck on the motorway grinding its gears. Soon we realised that it wasn't a truck at all, but a gigantic plane only just above the trees. We couldn't believe it when the plane just seemed to sink on to the motorway. Perhaps the pilot was trying to land there, but he had to turn sharply at the last moment and the plane nose-dived into the opposite bank. It was horrible. There was no explosion, luckily, so we went down to see what we could do to help. Terry – that's my boyfriend – rang from one of those emergency telephones on the side of the motorway."

6 You speak to the policeman in charge of the operation, Chief Inspector Patel, who tells you that the crash happened at 3.30 p.m.; that the plane was a regular flight from London (Stansted) to Oslo; and that so far 34 people have been rescued, with varying injuries, from the plane. He says that there is a danger of the fuel tanks exploding and that he must hurry on with his work. Many people are still trapped inside the plane, and in cars on the motorway.

7 In talking to one of the airline officials who has just arrived on the scene, you discover that this plane is Flight 002 and left Stansted at 3.10 p.m. this afternoon. You can see on the fuselage the name of the airline: Northeast Airlines.

8 You also manage to talk with one of the lucky escapees from a car which has plunged into the crash barriers in the middle of the motorway. He is Mr Kingsley Message, on his way from London to King's Lynn. "I don't know what Ethel will say when she hears about this. Ethel's my wife by the way. She'll be beside herself. Can you get a message to her? I'd be very grateful. Anyway, I was driving in the inside lane at about 45 mph when suddenly I saw this plane – about the size of ten or fifteen tankers – looking like it was going to land on the road in front of me. I was petrified, I can tell you. So I swerved off the road and then back on to it, ending up crashing into the barrier and spinning round so that I was facing the way I had come. It was lucky I had my seat-belt on. I don't know what I'm going to do now. My car's a write-off."

9 When you look at your watch again it is 4.15 p.m. You telephone your editor.

Your editor tells you that you can use between 400 and 500 words for your report, and that you have just under an hour to write it.

When you get back to the newspaper office at about 6 p.m., the report (which you telephoned through) is already set up for the evening edition. The sub-editor asks you to provide a banner headline, a sub-head of 8 to 12 words, and two or three interim headings to break up the report (e.g. 'Fuel-tank threat').

The bare facts

The following story appeared in the *Sevenoaks Chronicle* in August 1988. On this page, however, the opening paragraph of the story has been left out for you to reconstruct from the rest of the report.

First paragraphs in newspaper articles often summarise the important facts of the event. In this case, the opening paragraph ran to 29 words. Can you write a suitable opening paragraph of about that length?

When you have done that, put yourself in the shoes of an editor of a national newspaper who wants to include this story, but can only afford to give it between 100 and 120 words of space. Rewrite the report for a national audience.

Man flees naked from house to raise alarm

by Jackie Lindsay

The attempted robbery at The Avenue, Westerham Hill, home of Mr Michael Millward, came two years after a similar incident when three robbers made off with more than £80,000 worth of jewellery. Mr Millward had been beaten up and threatened with a shotgun.

Since that incident Mr Millward, aged 53, had slept behind a locked bedroom door, but unlocked it on Friday morning just before 2am to investigate the noise of a creaking footboard that he had heard in the hall.

Before opening the door, instinct had made him pick up a small Scottish sock knife, which he kept in his room.

"As I entered the hall, one individual dressed in black lunged at me. I stepped back and I felt I could not lose the initiative so I went forward and stabbed him in the right chest a minimum of three and perhaps four times," Mr Millward said.

The injured person did not move but Mr Millward saw two others appear from the darkness of the hall. He quickly retreated into his en suite bathroom and locked the door.

While the intruders were calling for Mr Millward to come out of the bathroom from the bedroom, he yelled for the police from the bathroom window. His house, however, stands in seclusion in five acres of land at the top of

Westerham Hill.

When he could no longer hear noises from the bedroom, he decided it was time to escape. "I thought I would take the undignified way out. I climbed out of the bathroom window, slid down the roof above the porch and hit the guttering which I hoped would hold," he said.

It did not and Mr Millward landed awkwardly on the ground, still completely naked.

He went to his car where he had left the keys in the ignition and also found a tracksuit in there. He had intended to drive to the police station but saw that Wolfe's Garage in Westerham was open when he drove past and stopped there to call the police.

When he returned to his house with the police, there was no sign of anyone but the intruders had left a hammer, a revolver, a cap and a ladder.

Mr Millward said the intruders had entered the house through a first floor hall window which had been left open because of the heat. He added that there had been a weak spot in his house-alarm system so it had not gone off. He believed they had left the way they had come and said there had been speculation that they may have had a car across the field.

In his bedroom, he discovered that

two of his shotguns, kept in a gun cabinet in there, had been stolen. One of these was a semi-automatic shotgun which he used for clay pigeon shooting.

"It would be disgusting in the wrong hands," he said. He added that there had been blood everywhere from the person he had stabbed.

He said he presumed that the three intruders were all men but could not be certain as they were all wearing balaclava helmets. He had not realised they had been armed with the hammer and revolver until their discovery with the ladder, but had still been frightened for his life.

"I really thought that I was going to meet my maker, especially when I ran from the other two," he said, "It was not that I was injured but it was the fact that there were three of them and I did not know where to go."

"I do not like living in a state of seige but I would prefer to do that and protect my home," he said. "I am nervous but I am not looking over my shoulder the whole time. This is my home and I am not going to be chased out."

Mr Millward is divorced with two children and was alone in the house on Thursday night. He moved into his house in 1976 and had been a gold bullion dealer in London for 20 years.

FROM STORYTELLING TO STORY WRITING

Story-time

Part 1

On this sheet is the transcript (the written-out version) of a story told by a third-year student in a London school. He told the story to a group of friends in an English lesson. The story was recorded, played back to the rest of the class and then transcribed.

> 'When we lived in this really long street, in a really old house, there was this warehouse across the street – a great white thing. It looked like marble but it wasn't marble – it had pillars and all that. It was deserted. It had these big steps leading up to it – it looked like a church but it wasn't. It might have been once.
>
> There were a load of places to hide around there, and there was this green gate you'd go over to get round the back. So a couple of these kids went over there and tried to get inside. They came back and said 'Oh yeh, we can get inside.' We all went over there: me, this other kid and his sister, we climbed over there, and the kids put their arm throught the door, like a grate, opened it, and went in. It was day but it was dark. We went through into this big main hall. There were no lights. We were dead scared, except that these two older kids had showed us how to get in there.
>
> It was really big, really gigantic – but, you know, I probably thought at the time that it was bigger than it really was. But really really HUGE! There were just windows at the top, you know. There were planks of wood and broken glass on the floor; we wondered what it was for. There were rats in there too. The older kids went out right quick and left us three in there. We were scared, but it got lighter after a couple of minutes. . .'
>
> **Jimmy**

Work in small groups. Take turns to tell stories of your own. Each group will need a tape-recorder and a quiet part of the school to work in.

The stories can be:

- anecdotes (i.e. tales of things you have done or that have happened to you);
- stories you have been told;
- stories you have read and can retell;
- folk stories you have heard or read.

Story-time

Part 2

Jimmy, the student in the school in London, was asked by his teacher to **write** the story that he told – not to write it out, but to write it as if he was writing that story for the first time. The aim was to produce a really good written story. Here is what Jimmy wrote.

I used to live on a long street called Pigott Street. It led diagonally away from the junction of Burdett Road and East India Dock Road. Old, three storey houses lined both sides of the road except for one, deserted warehouse which loomed way above even the houses. It was made of white, marble-like blocks which had the marks of slow condensation dripping down. Grey pigeons always sat on the crossing slab between two thick pillars. It looked quite like a large, old church except for the big red and white sign, 'Turnbull & Co' on the top. Eight foot studded doors were closed with four massive padlocks. A wide flight of steps led up to the door and these gave the warehouse its name, 'The Steps'.

The front of the warehouse was constructed with many holes and oddly shaped protrusions which were great for hide-and-seek, but no one ever actually went inside it. There were rumours of ghosts and bats and suchlike.

There were two boys; that must have been twelve or thirteen compared to my age, six; that climbed over the tall green fence, joining the warehouse to the row of houses, and came reporting back that they had been able to get inside.

A few days later, we – that is, my friend Paul, his sister Sheila and I – met the two boys, Geoff and Sunil at 'The Steps'. The sky was quite cloudy and it was one of those days when there is no wind which makes it seem really hot. The only sound was of the traffic on the main road, and this seemed less than usual. We were all pretty bored, when Geoff suggested, "Go in there again, shall we?"

"No," said Sunil quickly, "I ain't goin' in there again."
"Scared?"
"You know I ain't."
"Well come on then."
Now I complained, "Oh don't go, what'll we do then?"
"I s'pose you can come."

Geoff climbed first, straining a bit to get over, then he had to sit on a three inch ledge to help Paul, Sheila and myself over. Sunil came over last. I don't think he wanted to, but Geoff kept telling him to. In the small yard, shadowed by the adjoining house, everything was quite still. The dust of years was layered on all surfaces here, where no wind could reach. A few yards along the warehouse wall, there was a door, made of wood, but covered by a metal grating.

Nobody spoke or even whispered though there was no need for silence. Guilt disturbed me; it was like waking a sleeper. Sunil, who had thin arms, put his arm through the edge of the grating and sprung the latch. The door opened noiselessly on to the main part of the warehouse. The darkness was complete. As I stood on the threshold, the world was split in two; dark and light, but soon my eyes became accustomed and I began to see the vague outlines of enormous walls. The air was cold and smelt old. Planks of wood littered the floor and really gave the hall a derelict feeling. Suddenly, I was worried about its stability but remembered the sturdy pillars outside. Two tiny windows were set high up in the front wall but they shed little light on the scene I surveyed. We all stood quite close to the door just looking, then I realised Sunil and Geoff were gone. The door swung to, on its inclined hinges and reduced the opening to a mere crack. Paul gripped his sister's hand and I froze, alert, and ready for anything. Even in nine year-old Sheila's voice there was some shakiness as she said,
"Come on."

We walked slowly and stealthily towards the door, jumping at every scrape of wood on the floor, until eventually we reached it. Sheila flung it open and I breathed a sigh of relief then spun round realising I had my back to the darkness. Climbing up the crossbars of the fence, I knew I'd never see the inside of the warehouse again.

Put the two versions of the story side by side, and see how many differences you can spot. Discuss with a partner. Why do you think there are these differences?

Now write the story that your group told to the rest of the class. Try to produce a really good written story.

Behind the scenes

Read the story *Becky and the Wheels-and-brake Boys* by James Berry. You might want to listen to it read first, then read it again to yourself.

This seems to be a good story to turn into a script for recording, like the short stories that are turned into plays for the radio or for television. The work would have to be done in several stages.

First, break the story into nine or ten '**scenes**'. See if you can identify each change of scene, and draw a line across the text where each one occurs. The different scenes should be listed and agreed on before any further writing takes place.

Now, in collaboration with your teacher, and working in groups of two or three, you need to decide which scene you will be working on.

Next comes the difficult part. Working together, you have to 'translate' the story into play-form. Plays, as you know, are composed largely of **dialogue** (*two* or more people speaking), with some **monologue** (*one* person speaking), and **stage directions** and/or **sound effects**. Some scenes in the original story have more dialogue than others: these will be easier to make into script than scenes without much dialogue, but you should still aim to create some *new* dialogue for your particular scene.

If you are working on a scene with little or no dialogue in the story, you should either write it in monologue from Becky, or create a character for her to share her thoughts with.

As you write, you will be faced with different problems that you should try and solve together in your small groups. ***Don't give up:*** remember your job is to lift the story 'off the page' and make it into a play.

When everyone has completed their part, the play can be performed, either 'live' or on tape for playback later, with one scene following another as in the story.

Behind the scenes

Becky and the Wheels-and-brake Boys

Even my own cousin Ben was there – riding away, in the ringing of bicycle bells down the road. Every time I came to watch them – see them riding round and round enjoying themselves – they scooted off like crazy on their bikes.

They can't keep doing that. They'll see!

I only want to be with Nat, Aldo, Jimmy and Ben. It's no fair reason they don't want to be with me. Anybody could go off their head for that. Anybody! A girl can not, not, let boys get away with it all the time.

Bother! I have to walk back home, alone.

I know total-total that if I had my own bike, the Wheels-and-brake Boys wouldn't treat me like that. I'd just ride away with them, wouldn't I?

Over and over I told my mum I wanted a bike. Over and over she looked at me as if I was crazy. "Becky, d'you think you're a boy? Eh? D'you think you're a boy? In any case, where's the money to come from? Eh?"

Of course I know I'm not a boy. Of course I know I'm not crazy. Of course I know all that's no reason why I can't have a bike. No reason! As soon as I get indoors I'll just have to ask again – ask Mum once more.

At home, indoors, I didn't ask my mum.

It was evening time, but sunshine was still big patches in yards and on housetops. My two younger brothers, Lenny and Vin played marbles in the road. Mum was taking measurements of a boy I knew, for his new trousers and shirt. Mum made clothes for people. Meggie, my sister two years younger than me, was helping Mum on the verandah. Nobody would be pleased with me not helping. I began to help.

Granny-Liz would always stop fanning herself to drink up a glass of iced water. I gave my granny a glass of iced water, there in her rocking-chair. I looked in the kitchen to find shelled coconut pieces to cut into small cubes for the fowls' morning feed. But Granny-Liz had done it. I came and started tidying up bits and pieces of cut-off material around my mum on the floor. My sister got nasty, saying she was already helping Mum. Not a single good thing was happening for me.

With me even being all so thoughtful of Granny's need of a cool drink, she started up some botheration against me.

Listen to Granny-Liz: "Becky, with you moving about me here on the verandah, I hope you don't have any centipedes or scorpions in a jam jar in your pocket."

"No, mam," I said sighing, trying to be calm. "Granny-Liz," I went on, "you forgot. My centipede and scorpion died." All the same, storm broke against me.

"Becky," my mum said. "You know I don't like you wandering off after dinner. Haven't I told you I don't want you keeping company with those awful riding-about bicycle boys? Eh?"

"Yes, mam."

"Those boys are a menace. Riding bicycles on sidewalks and narrow paths together, ringing bicycle bells and braking at people's feet like wild bulls charging anybody, they're heading for trouble."

"They're the Wheels-and-brake Boys, mam."

"The what?"

"The Wheels-and-brake Boys."

"Oh! Given themselves a name as well, have they? Well, Becky, answer this. How d'you always manage to look like you've just escaped from a hair-pulling battle? Eh? And don't I tell you not to break the back down and wear your canvas shoes like slippers? Don't you ever hear what I say?"

"Yes, mam."

"D'you want to end up a field labourer? Like where your father used to be overseer?"

"No, mam."

"Well, Becky, will you please go off and do your homework?"

Everybody did everything to stop me. I was allowed no chance whatsoever. No chance to talk to Mum about the bike I dream of day and night! And I knew exactly the bike I wanted. I wanted a bike like Ben's bike. Oh, I wished I still had even my scorpion on a string to run up and down somebody's back!

I answered my mum. "Yes, mam." I went off into Meg's and my bedroom.

I sat down at the little table, as well I might. Could homework stay in anybody's head in broad daylight outside? No. Could I keep a bike like Ben's out of my head? Not one bit. That bike took me all over the place. My beautiful bike jumped every log, every rock, every fence. My beautiful bike did everything cleverer than a clever cowboy's horse, with me in the saddle. And the bell, the bell was such a glorious gong of a ring!

If Dad was alive I could talk to him. If Dad was alive he'd give me money for the bike like a shot.

I sighed. It was amazing what a sigh could do. I sighed and tumbled on a great idea. Tomorrow evening I'd get Shirnette to come with me. Both of us together would be sure to get the boys interested to teach us to ride. Wow! With Shirnette they can't just ride away!

Behind the scenes

the story continued . . .

Next day at school everything went sour. For the first time, Shirnette and me had a real fight, because of what I hated most.

Shirnette brought a cockroach to school in a shoe-polish tin. At playtime she opened the tin and let the cockroach fly into my blouse. Pure panic and disgust nearly killed me. I crushed up the cockroach in my clothes and practically ripped my blouse off, there in open sunlight. Oh the smell of a cockroach is the nastiest ever to block your nose! I started running with my blouse to go and wash it. Twice I had to stop and be sick.

I washed away the crushed cockroach stain from my blouse. Then the stupid Shirnette had to come into the toilet, falling about laughing. All right, I knew the cockroach treatment was for the time when I made my centipede on a string crawl up Shirnette's back. But you put fair-is-fair aside. I just barged into Shirnette.

When it was all over I had on a wet blouse, but Shirnette had one on too.

Then going home with the noisy flock of children from school I had ever such a new, new idea. If Mum thought I was scruffy, Nat, Aldo, Jimmy and Ben might think so too. I didn't like that.

After dinner, I combed my hair in the bedroom. Mum did her machining on the verandah. Meggie helped Mum. Granny sat there, wishing she could take on any job, as usual.

I told Mum I was going to make up a quarrel with Shirnette. I went, but my friend wouldn't speak to me, let alone come out to keep me company. I stood alone and watched the Wheels-and-brake Boys again.

This time the boys didn't race away past me. I stood leaning against the tall coconut palm tree. People passed up and down. The nearby main road was busy with traffic. But I didn't mind. I watched the boys. Riding round and round the big Flame-tree, Nat, Aldo, Jimmy and Ben looked marvellous.

At first each boy rode round the tree alone. Then each boy raced each other round the tree, going round three times. As he won, the winner rang his bell on and on, till he stopped panting and could laugh and talk properly. Next, most reckless and fierce, all the boys raced against each other. And, leaning against their bicycles, talking and joking, the boys popped soft drinks open, drank and ate chipped bananas.

I walked up to Nat, Aldo, Jimmy and Ben and said, "Can somebody teach me to ride?"

"Why don't you stay indoors and learn to cook and sew and wash clothes?" Jimmy said.

I grinned. "I know all that already," I said. "And one day perhaps I'll even be mum to a boy child, like all of you. Can you cook and sew and wash clothes, Jimmy? All I want is to learn to ride. I want you to teach me."

I didn't know why I said what I said. But everybody went silent and serious.

One after the other, Nat, Aldo, Jimmy and Ben got on to their bikes and rode off. I wasn't at all cross with them. I only wanted to be riding out of the playground with them. I knew they'd be heading into the town to have ice-cream and things and talk and laugh.

Mum was sitting alone on the verandah. She sewed buttons on to a white shirt she'd made. I sat down next to Mum. Straightaway, "Mum," I said, "I still want to have a bike badly."

"Oh, Becky, you still have that foolishness in your head? What am I going to do?"

Mum talked with some sympathy. Mum knew I was honest. "I can't get rid of it, mam," I said.

Mum stopped sewing. "Becky," she said, staring in my face, "how many girls around here do you see with bicycles?"

"Janice Gordon has a bike," I reminded her.

"Janice Gordon's dad has acres and acres of coconuts and bananas, with a business in the town as well."

I knew Mum was just about to give in. Then my granny had to come out on to the verandah and interfere. Listen to that Granny-Liz. "Becky, I heard your mother tell you over and over she can't afford to buy you a bike. Yet you keep on and on. Child, you're a girl."

"But I don't want a bike because I'm a girl."

"D'you want it because you feel like a boy?" Granny said.

"No. I only want a bike because I want it and want it and want it."

Granny just carried on. "A tomboy's like a whistling woman and a crowing hen, who can only come to a bad end. D'you understand?"

I didn't want to understand. I knew Granny's speech was an awful speech. I went and sat down with Lenny and Vin, who were making a kite.

By Saturday morning I felt real sorry for Mum. I could see Mum really had it hard for money. I had to try and help. I knew anything of Dad's – anything – would be worth a great mighty hundred pounds.

Behind the scenes

the story continued . . .

I found myself in the centre of town, going through the busy Saturday crowd. I hoped Mum wouldn't be too cross. I went into the fire station. With lots of luck I came face to face with a round face man in uniform. He talked to me. "Little miss, can I help you?"

I told him I'd like to talk to the head man. He took me into the office and gave me a chair. I sat down. I opened out my brown paper parcel. I showed him my dad's sun helmet. I told him I thought it would make a good fireman's hat. I wanted to sell the helmet for some money towards a bike, I told him.

The fireman laughed a lot. I began to laugh too. The fireman put me in a car and drove me back home.

Mum's eyes popped to see me bringing home the fireman. The round face fireman laughed at my adventure. Mum laughed too, which was really good. The fireman gave Mum my dad's hat back. Then, mystery, mystery, Mum sent me outside while they talked.

My mum was only a little cross with me. Then – mystery and more mystery – my mum took me with the fireman in his car to his house.

The fireman brought out what? A bicycle! A beautiful, shining bicycle! His nephew's bike. His nephew had been taken away, all the way to America. The bike had been left with the fireman-uncle for him to sell it. And the good kind fireman-uncle decided we could have the bike – on small payments. My mum looked uncertain. But, in a big, big way the fireman knew it was all right. And Mum smiled a little. My Mum had good sense to know it was all right. My Mum took the bike from the fireman Mister Dean.

And guess what? Seeing my bike much, much newer than his, my cousin Ben's eyes popped with envy. But – he took on the big job. He taught me to ride. Then he taught Shirnette.

I ride into town with the Wheels-and-brake Boys now. When she can borrow a bike, Shirnette comes too. We all sit together. We have patties and ice-cream and drink drinks together. We talk and joke. We ride about, all over the place.

And, again, guess what? Fireman Mister Dean became our best friend, and Mum's especially. He started coming round almost everyday.

REPORT 2

Going National!

Here are two reports from *The Beverley Guardian*, from their Chief Reporter, Mark Wilford. How would you report both stories for (*a*) *The Daily Mirror*, (*b*) *The Independent*, given half the space that each of the reports are allowed here?

You might find it useful to take a coloured pen and underline parts of the local reports which you think you will keep. You will then have to put these in a suitable order, and adjust length and style to suit the different audiences of *The Mirror* and *The Independent*.

MERCY FLIGHT

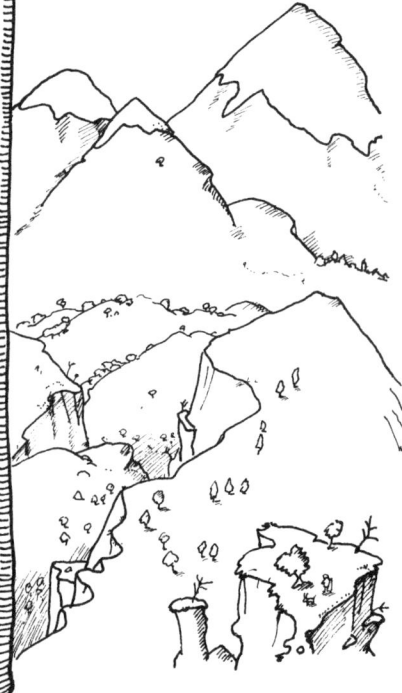

Beverley doctors Peter and Beryl Beynon expect to fly into the red-hot cauldron of Afghanistan within the next 10 days on a desperate life saving mercy mission.

They hope to fly to Kabul to meet up with three tonnes of medical aid sent out earlier this week, but the container has become stuck in Prague after the courier expected to fly with it was refused a seat on the plane.

"Although we had got telephone confirmation from the United Nations that a visa would be issued in Kabul I did not have any written permission for him and now the container is stuck in Prague," said Dr Beryl Beynon.

"It's unlikely to be this week when we leave but it could be the following weekend when we go," she added. "I have to wait until I receive news that it has arrived in Kabul."

Dr Beynon has also heard that two more couriers have been given permission to take medicines by plane but it is not known when they will leave.

The worsening political situation in the country, likely to degenerate into all-out civil war when the Russian troops complete their withdrawal to leave the Government at the mercy of the Mujahadeen rebels, has forced the British Embassy to close in Kabul.

Britons are being advised not to go but Dr Beynon is determined to go ahead with the trip, even though the fear remains that if she does arrive in Kabul the airport may be closed preventing any escape.

"It's a very necessary trip but I shall be relieved to get back. The main problem is the airport. We shall know it is open when we leave London but after that we will have no idea," she said.

There are only two flights a week to Kabul, one via Moscow and the other via Prague and no aid has been sent from this country to the main hospitals. The only help is from the International Red Cross for its own small hospital in the city.

Going National!

Call to remove age limit on drinks

Beverley publicans' leader has called for new laws abolishing the age limit on drinking after new figures revealed that under-age drinking in the town's pubs is rife.

Mr Alan Harvie, president of the town's Licensed Victuallers' Association, said it was time the Government looked seriously at removing the age limit and bringing the country into line with other European nations.

Although the town's new identity card scheme has helped in stopping youngsters drinking illegally, Mr Harvie said the problem would never clear up entirely and was putting landlord's livelihoods under threat.

New legislation means that if landlords are found to have broken the strict laws about selling alcohol to under-age drinkers, two prosecutions could result in their losing their licences.

Richard Hildyard, a schoolboy member of the town's crime prevention panel, also supports the removal of the limit and Mr Harvie said he hoped to put the point forward to Beverley MP Mr Jim Cran at a future meeting.

Mr Harvie said he did not believe the situation was as bad as police figures indicated and suggested that the increase in prosecutions for under-age drinking was due to increased police activity.

Supt Bob Carmichael told Beverley's licensing justices that last year there were 17 prosecutions and 12 cautions for under-age drinking compared with only three prosecutions in 1987.

He warned that publicans' efforts to cut down on under-age drinking were admirable but the ID card scheme did not include off-licences and supermarkets and their vigilance could divert youngsters to other sources of drink.

Mr Carmichael said the extended drinking hours brought in during August had not led to increased public order and drunkenness problems, with the attraction of Beverley for all day drinking on Saturdays now shared with other towns.

REPORT 3

Editorial changes

Shaun Slater works for a small local paper in Yorkshire, *The Beverley Guardian*. This is the report he typed for the front page of the paper one week:

A close shave for Beverley landlord Steve Dearing caused a mix-up at the town's Westwood Hospital that almost left it missing out on a charity windfall.

Steve, who runs the Lord Nelson, was to have given the £150 he raised from a sponsored haircut to the hospital's baby unit. But after hearing they had enough money he considered handing over to another charity.

A phone call to the hospital baffled officials who said they were always happy to have more funds and the problem was solved. Steve said he would be presenting the unit with a cheque that would be put towards the unit's cardiorator appeal. The cardiorator helps detect heart defects in infants and has been responsible for saving many lives.

Of the haircut Steve said: "I've had it done before when I worked in a Howden pub and this time it's not quite so short. I get a few funny looks in the street but at least it will grow back in two or three months."

Steve's wife Tina apparently does not mind his skinhead look and two of his friends, Lyndon Carling and Richard Holgate, were so impressed with Matthew Wordsworth's shaving skills they followed Steve's example.

Explaining why he had gone for the drastic cut, Steve said: "Big Bill, who's a barman in the pub, said he would go on a sponsored diet but after a couple of days he gave up. I thought I better do something instead and all I could think of was having my hair shaved. At least it's one way of getting a free haircut."

And here is the report as it appeared in the newspaper.

- What changes have been made?
- Give the story a new headline.
- Can you give four sub-headings (one for each paragraph) to break up the text?

If you had been the editor of the newspaper, would you have made these changes? If not, what changes would you have made? (Would you, for example, rearrange the *original* sequence of paragraphs?)

A close shave for hospital

A close shave for Beverley landlord Steve Dearing caused a mix-up at the town's Westwood Hospital that almost left it missing out on a charity windfall.

Steve, who runs the Lord Nelson in Flemingate was to have given the £150 he raised from a sponsored haircut to the hospital's baby unit, but after hearing they had enough he considered handing it over to another charity.

A phone call to the hospital baffled officials who said they were always happy to have more funds and the problem was solved. Steve said he would present the unit with the cheque to be put towards its cardiorator appeal. The cardiorator will detect heart defects in infants and could save many lives.

Of the haircut Steve said: "I've had it done before when I worked in a Howden pub and this time it's not quite so short. I get a few funny looks in the street but at least it will grow back in two or three months."

Getting into print

Much travel writing for guide books is done on location and is written up later for publication. Here is some material written on a lap-top wordprocessor by John Noble. Imagine you are the editor of a guide to Mexico, and have decided to use this material in the introduction to the book. How would you change it?

Mexico is an extraordinarily diverse country — in culture, mood, customs and history. This goes back to pre-Hispanic times when there were often several different civilisations in different areas at the same time, and it's largely a result of Mexico's rugged geography. Cortés, asked to describe the map of Mexico, simply crumpled up a piece of paper and laid it on the table, and the mountains which still isolate different parts of the country from each other make Mexico in a sense much bigger than it looks. Communications are much slower than in western countries, which helps to preserve the separate identities of each region. To go for instance the 200 km from hot, coastal, musical Veracruz to the quiet, dry mountain fastnesses of Oaxaca is to enter a different world. Mexico is truly many Mexicos — at one extreme are the superficially westernised city middle classes, at the other the 50-plus Indian peoples, each with their own language, scattered over the remotest parts of the country. In between are the distinct characters of the mestizo — mixed blood populations of each region, each with a strong pride in their own land, cooking, music, festivals, and traditions. Like every really intriguing place, Mexico's a country where the more you learn, the less you realise you know.

Write out your edited version, and then compare it with the text which actually appeared in *The Lonely Planet Guide to Mexico*:

Mexico's extraordinary diversity goes back to pre-Hispanic times when several civilisations often occupied the country at the same time. It's also largely a result of the rugged geography. Cortés, asked to describe the map of Mexico, crumpled up a piece of paper and laid it on a table.

The mountains which isolate parts of the country make Mexico a much bigger country to travel through than it may appear on the map. Communications are much slower than in western countries, which helps preserve the separate identities of each region. To go for instance the 200 km from hot, coastal, music-loving Veracruz to the dry, quiet mountain fastnesses of Oaxaca is to travel to a different world.

As for the people of Mexico, at one extreme are the superficially westernised middle classes of the cities, at the other the 50-plus Indian peoples, each with their own language, scattered over the remotest parts of the country. Between the two are the mestizo (mixed blood) populations, each with a strong pride in its traditions.

Land of many faces, Mexico is a country where the more you learn, the more you realise how little you knew.

STYLE

In 1947, Raymond Queneau published a book called *Exercices de Style* (translated into English as *Exercises in Style*), in which he tells the same minimal story over one hundred times and in as many different ways. Here is the basic story which, in the book, comes under the heading of 'Notation'.

A matter of *Style!*

In the S bus, in the rush hour. A chap of about 26, felt hat with a cord instead of a ribbon, neck too long, as if someone's been having a tug-of-war with it. People getting off. The chap in question gets annoyed with one of the men standing next to him. He accuses him of jostling him every time anyone goes past. A snivelling tone which is meant to be aggressive. When he sees a vacant seat he throws himself on to it.

Two hours later, I meet him in the Cour de Rome, in front of the gare Saint-Lazare. He's with a friend who's saying: "You ought to get an extra button put on your overcoat." He shows him where (at the lapels) and why.

And here is the same story told in another way:

I beg to advise you of the following facts of which I happened to be the equally impartial and horrified witness.

Today, at roughly twelve noon, I was present on the platform of a bus which was proceeding up the rue de Courcelles in the direction of the Place Champerret. The aforementioned bus was fully laden – more than fully laden, I might even venture to say, since the conductor had accepted an overload of several candidates, without valid reason and actuated by an exaggerated kindness of heart which caused him to exceed the regulations and which, consequently, bordered on indulgence. At each stopping place the perambulations of the outgoing and incoming passengers did not fail to provoke a certain disturbance which incited one of these passengers to protest, though not without timidity. I should mention that he went and sat down as and when this eventuality became possible.

I will append to this short account this addendum: I had occasion to observe this passenger some time subsequently in the company of an individual whom I was unable to identify. The conversation which they were exchanging with some animation seemed to have a bearing on questions of an aesthetic nature.

In view of these circumstances, I would request you to be so kind, Sir, as to intimate to me the inference which I should draw from these facts and the attitude which you would then deem appropriate that I adopt in re the conduct of my subsequent mode of life.

Anticipating the favour of your reply, believe me to be, Sir, your very obedient servant at least.

A matter of
Style!

Queneau also tells this story in the following styles:

- *in surprise*
- *as a dream*
- *with hesitation*
- *precisely (with precise measurements, times, etc.)*
- *in anagrams*
- *in the past tense*
- *in Cockney*
- *awkwardly*
- *casually*
- *in a biased way*

Now **you** try writing in a variety of styles. You can either make up your own bare bones of a story, or use Queneau's. Other styles which you might like to try, in addition to some of those listed already, are:

- *tabloid newspaper*
- *'quality' press*
- *holiday brochure*
- *estate agents' particulars*
- *commentary (e.g. sports commentary)*
- *interview*
- *TV chat show*
- *conspiratorial*
- *legal*
- *public announcement*
- *scientific write-up (e.g. lab. report)*

INTERVIEWS 1

Tell me about it

Imagine you are a reporter on the *Freetown Gazette*. One morning you get a call from the Chief Editor who tells you that you have a choice: either you can interview Sally Woolfe, who has just come back from a schools expedition to the Himalayas, and who had to return early because of a broken leg; or you can interview Tony Walker, who has just been picked for the England under-21 soccer team after attending the Football Associations's school of excellence for promising young players.

Decide which of the interviews you will do. Write down between six and ten questions that you will ask.

Now pair up with another member of your class. Play the parts of the interviewer and the interviewee, and then swop roles.

When you act as interviewer, try to let the interviewee say as much as possible. Get him or her talking, and either note down the basic points as fast as you can, or record the conversation on tape.

When you act as the interviewee, give long answers to the questions. Remember that the newspaper wants to find out as much about you as it can.

If you tape your interview, you have a long but interesting job ahead of you. Take the tape home and transcribe (i.e. write out) the conversation. From this conversation, select certain parts which you think will form the basis of an interesting article – most of which will be in reported speech, but some of which can be direct quotations from the interview.

If you have simply made notes on the conversation, work from these to produce a short article for the newspaper.

Meeting point

This is your chance to conduct a real interview with someone who interests you, either in school or in the wider community, for example:

- one of the dinner helpers
- the school librarian
- the caretaker
- the Head or one of the deputies
- one of the teachers
- one of the pupils
- a school governor
- a local policeman or policewoman
- a traffic warden
- someone who works in local radio
- a postman or postwoman
- the milkman/woman
- someone in a local shop
- someone involved in a campaign

You may have to write a letter first to ask permission to conduct the interview.

When the time for the interview has been arranged (you will probably need about half an hour), confirm it and make sure you are punctual. Take a taperecorder with you and ask permission to use it.

At the interview

Your opening questions should put the interviewee at ease. After that, you can move beyond your prepared questions if you feel that the conversation is going well. Remember that a good interview should be more like a conversation than a formal question-and-answer session.

When you have completed the interview and thanked the interviewee, take the tape home and transcribe the conversation. This will take some time, but it is worth having a written record.

Then select from the transcript the parts of the interview that you want to write up in article form. This may involve changing the sequence of some of the material and shifting some of it into the past tense and into reported-speech form. You may want to write an introductory 'portrait' of the person interviewed.

When everyone in the class has completed his or her article, collect them and display or publish!

REWRITING FOR YOUNGER CHILDREN

Think about your readers

Here is an extract from a guide written for teenagers about how to look after themselves in the holidays. See if you can rewrite it for nine to ten year olds. You might have to change some of the content as well as the language in which the guide is written.

Doing things

One way to keep out of trouble is to keep active and get involved in projects, expeditions and schemes that are running in your area. There might be a scheme to plant trees around the neighbourhood, or the chance to go away camping with a local Scout or Guide group; the local council might want helpers to design and paint a mural on a blank wall, or there might be a scheme to help the elderly in the community. Don't just lie in bed watching television or listening to that tape again and again! Do something!

Looking after yourself

You've been told countless times as a young child, "Don't talk to strangers." But there are other ways – some of them more positive – of looking after yourself. One rule is to operate in groups. If you want to explore the woods on the edge of town or mess around on the beach, stick together. Don't get into situations where one of you is stranded or left alone. Wear clothes that enable you to run if you have to: be streetwise, and be prepared to help out anyone (young or old) who seems to be in trouble.

Be prepared

You don't have to be a Scout or Guide to be prepared. Always carry enough money with you to make a few phonecalls or pay for a busride home; if you're on a bike, make sure you have a repair kit with you. And what if it pours down suddenly? Have you got something you can put on so that you don't get soaked? Don't push yourself too far, like climbing up a wall you know you can't scale, or getting too far from home. Make sure you know what the time is and where your responsibilities lie.

★ First decide whether you want to include all the information here – you could underline what you want to keep in a coloured pen. Then discuss what else you think you should include that isn't mentioned here.

★ Now organise your material into a suitable sequence. Decide whether you are going to present it as a poster, a booklet, or in some other format.

★ Are you going to use illustrations? Are any of the words too difficult for 9 to 10 year olds? Are any of the sentences too long or difficult to understand?

A very strange case

Sitting at police headquarters, you receive a phone call to say that a crime has been committed on an industrial estate on the edge of town. All you have to go on are this phone call and a Polaroid photograph brought into the office by one of your staff.

Try to reconstruct the crime. You will have to use your imagination to invent the details of what could have happened, but you must also use the detail that appears in the photograph. Write out your reconstruction in draft form, either as a police report, as a story or as a list of events (with times).

A very strange case

Later in the day, a new photograph is brought into the office, taken by a bystander. It shows new evidence.

You have part of the photograph blown up to show the young person in more detail. What can you tell about the person? Might he or she be involved in the crime – or a witness to any incident?

Interview the person and/or rewrite your notes/report/story to take account of this new development. You could develop this activity into a full-scale trial in which the person in the photograph gives evidence (either as the accused or as a witness). . .

Selling off the page

You have been given the job of writing a company's brochure, reporting on its achievements and aiming, in the long run, to persuade the readers of the brochure to use the company's services. What is needed is about 300 words, including some facts but generally introducing the reader to the company and what it does.

Here are a few facts that you might want to use.

- The company, Insulite plc (Public Limited Company), makes especially light-weight insulation for lining pipes, roof spaces, vehicles (like cars, jet aircraft and space rockets) and clothing.

- The product, Insulite, has been recently created by scientists in the laboratories at the company. It is created by melting waste brick-rubble and concrete at very high temperatures, and then spinning fibres from that liquid. The fibres are compacted into whichever shape is required for the job in hand. The rest of the manufacturing process is secret.

- Insulite has factories in England, Scotland, France and Colombia.

- Insulite employs over 4000 people worldwide.

- Profits last year were up 14% on the previous year, and the company is expanding its operations with a new factory planned in Hong Kong.

- One example of the success of Insulite is the manufacture of a new kind of underwear. This is an all-in-one bodysuit that retains heat in cold weather and yet cools down the body in hot temperatures. It is so efficient that it has been used on polar expeditions as well as in treks across the Gobi and Sahara deserts.

- Another example of Insulite's achievement is in the cladding of the Hong Kong and Taiwan Bank headquarters in Hong Kong: this multi-million pound building is entirely lined with Insulite and is thought to be the world's best-insulated structure. Despite its size, it can be heated with a small paraffin stove.

- All Insulite's products are made without CFCs, and so are 'environment-friendly'. Insulite plc has a reputation for caring for the environment, as demonstrated by its recent sponsoring of the Green March from Rome to London, the aim of which was to raise public awareness of environmental issues.

You should select the pieces of information that you think are most appropriate, and then put them in an order which will convince the reader that Insulite is the product to buy. Experiment with the order until you think you've got it right. Invent more material if you wish.

You may like to make your brochure look more authentic by using cuttings from magazines, sketches and captions – and by presenting the material in a readable and appealing way.

REPORT 4

Time for order

Here is a report written for a local newspaper. Each paragraph has been numbered, for reference.

Sixteen-year-old heroine rescues family

1 Schoolgirl Sharon Westley climbed a 150-foot cliff near her home in East Yorkshire yesterday after her family was stranded on a beach by a freak incoming tide.

2 She raised the alarm by phoning from the farmhouse of Mr and Mrs Truelove of Skidelby Grange, who were unaware of the drama taking place down on the beach.

3 She climbed up the muddy chalk cliffs in about ten minutes and then communicated to her family in sign language that she was going to the farm to get help.

4 The Air-Sea Rescue Service was on the scene within minutes, winching Mr and Mrs Westley and their son Darren to safety before the tide covered the beach.

5 The family were holidaying at the caravan site at Washhaven and had gone to the beach for a picnic. They had not seen the warning in the local paper of high spring tides along the Yorkshire coast.

6 "Sharon has been on outward-bound courses with her school," said a relieved Trevor Westley, safe at the rescue station and sipping a cup of hot tea, "and that's probably where she learned to climb."

7 "She's a brave girl, and we owe her our lives," said her Mum.

8 Elsewhere on the coast, three students had tried to swim to safety when they realised the tide was exceptionally high. They were picked up by rescue helicopter and taken to Summerscale Hospital, suffering from cold and shock.

About the paragraphs

1 gives the basic outline of the story.
2 gives further details, including information about others involved in the incident.
3 goes back in time, filling in more detail.
4 moves forward in time, to the rescue itself.
5 fills in the background, going back in time.
6 is a quotation from the father, going back yet further in time.
7 is in the 'present'.
8 gives information about another (related) incident that happened at about the same time as the Westley incident.

Time for order

What to do

Cut up the report on sheet 38A into its eight paragraphs, and see if you can make it read just as well in different sequences. Record, by the numbers only, any sequences that don't work at all, and also those that you think are acceptable. Then decide which sequence you will put forward for discussion by the whole class, and stick down the paragraphs in that order on a sheet of paper.

Now try writing your own report that moves backwards and forwards in time, like the story about Sharon. Choose your own subject and aim for about eight short paragraphs. Provide a headline and try to include quotations from witnesses or those involved. Then see if you can alter the sequence of your report. Experiment until you have the order you think works best.

Analyse your own story, and others that you cut from newspapers, to see how they move about in time. Here is an example from *The Beverley Guardian* to start you off.

A Beverley woman has pledged to continue throwing her body before JCB excavators in a bid to save an ancient hedge from further "devastation" by builders.

Mrs Joanne Richardson, of Canterbury Close, is leading a group of residents incensed at the ripping up of part of a 100-year-old hedge between their gardens and adjoining land.

The work is being carried out by contractors for Minster Homes Ltd, who claim they have to remove the hedge to lay drainage pipes to honour an agreement with Beverley Borough Council.

Residents are angry at what they see as excessive and thoughtless destruction carried out, without prior warning, to the hedge, which stood 4ft deep and 13ft high.

"I went out at 2pm on Thursday and when I returned at four it was all over. There had been birds' nests and young fledglings in the hedge – it was slaughter. The JCB grabbed branches and just ripped them out," said Mrs Richardson.

She told how when the digger returned on following mornings, she stood before it to prevent its access to the hedge. She said: "We have got to do something to stop this. If we have to stand in front of a JCB to protect it, then we will stand in front of a JCB."

Mr Kevin Gill, who will move into a house in the close in three weeks' time with his wife and two young children, said the destruction had ruined his home's privacy and safety.

"I was totally shocked. I was devastated to think that in this day and age people can come and start taking away your garden. Before we had plenty of privacy. Now anyone can just walk into our garden," he said.

A spokesman for Minster Homes said the company was taking as much care as possible with the work. He said: "We are using a JCB and so we are catching some branches in the hedge, but we will be replacing the damaged parts. If a mature tree is knocked down, we will plant a mature one back, and a landscape gardener will be employed to trim everything back properly."

He added that the hedge was not owned by the residents, as their property boundary only went halfway into it, and that Beverley Borough Council's technical services department stated that it wanted the drainage pipe laying in the dry ditch beneath the bushes.

The council chief executive, Mr Jim Thomas, said he had been assured that the hedge would recover.

COPY EDITING

Dotting the 'i's

Much of the following story is badly expressed, badly structured and badly spelt. If you were working as an editor in a publishing house, what would you have to do to this manuscript to improve *it? The first few lines are edited for you to give you an idea of the kinds of comments you can make.*

(Don't forget about paragraphing!)

/⊙ (cap)

ℓ

(caps)

When she got out of bed that morning, Christina knew it was going to be an awful day for a start she couldn't decide what to eat for breakfast and ended up eating nothing. She gulped down a cup of cold black coffee and dragged herself out of the house towards the bus-stop. Three buses went past for sydenham, streatham and norwood, then she gave up and tried hitching a lift. To her amasement a driver stopped almost immediatley, he swung open the door and she felt herself drawn into the passenger seat before she could really stop and think 'What am I doing?', 'Should I be doing this?' and so on. As they sped into the centre of London past commuters on their way to work, passed newspaper sellers trying to hold down their papers in the wind, passed dogs roaming the streets, she turned to look at the man who had picked her up, he was about forty. His skin was open-pored and he had little hairs poking out from all sorts of places on his face. His teeth were yellow and mishapen, and he has hairs growing thickly on the back of each finger. She felt like jumping out of the car at that moment but at that moment they were travelling at about forty mph. When she got into the car she knew she shouldn't have but she couldn't hhelp herself. Now she was regreting it. 'Stop at these lights' she managed to squeeze out, trying to disgiuse the fact her voice was fast dissappearring, this is where I want to get off. The lights were green on no thpought Christina he's going to go through them. He went through them and didn't stop. In the next traffic jam, half a mile up the road, she broke out of the door when the car was traveling at about tem miles per hour. . .

Is this all you want to say at the beginning?

The art of selling

Take an A4 sheet of paper and fold it into three, like this. →

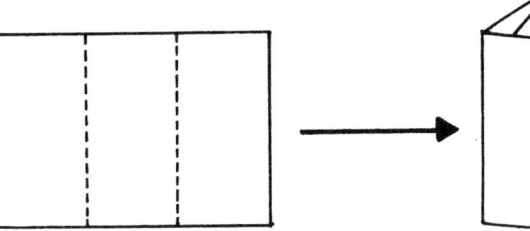

Think of a product you want to sell to your friends, like a newly designed fashion line or a service you can offer, like wordprocessing. Your job is to design a small brochure to advertise your company. Mostly, this brochure can consist of photographs (which you can cut from magazines), but it will need some written text too.

Here is an example of such a text from a brochure, using about 150 words. There is also a photograph you might want to use for *your* brochure.

Illumineering is a system of lighting which is derived from recycled, aesthetic machine parts. Each unit is individual and craftsman built, and combines practicality with an exclusive art form, giving its environment mood and texture with its intricate shadow effects.

The Illumineering range has been developed with an awareness to our ever diminishing supply of natural resources, producing originality not only in its use of innately beautiful materials, but also in its adaptation of these materials from one function to another.

Julian Kirk-Alton is a graduate of design technology who has had continued interest in energy and resource conservation. This combined with an unusual knack for taking component parts and putting them into entirely abstract situations has evolved into this most recent range of lighting.

ILLUMINEERING

ELIMINATING BIAS

Who was Ben Hall?

Ben Hall lived over a hundred years ago in the Australian outback. Here are two accounts of him: the first sees him as a likeable bushranger and 'gentleman thief', and the second as a dangerous outlaw. See if you can write an **unbiased** account of him for the local museum.

First, you will need to work through the two passages to identify the basic 'facts' around which you can construct the rest of your account. Use as much of the material as you can, and use a coloured pen to underline this information.

Arrange the material in a suitable order. Then, as you draft your account, choose your words carefully to eliminate any bias for or against Ben Hall.

Gentleman thief?

In the grey light of a new day, the blacktracker, Billy Dargin, crept towards the sleeping man in the gully.

A horse snorted, waking the man who struggled to his feet. Dargin shot him in the stomach . . .

So ended the life of Ben Hall, the first Australian bushranger to be outlawed. It was a sad end for a once respected member of the community. Ben Hall was born at Breeza, Liverpool Plains, in 1837, the son of convict parents.

He spent his early years at Murrurundi, where his father ran cattle. When the family moved to the Lachlan, ten year old Ben went with them. He helped his father on a station in the district until 1852 when the elder Hall returned to Murrurundi.

Young Ben Hall then leased a run at Wheogo, in the Grenfell district, where he gained a reputation for honesty, hard work and enterprise. He married Bridget (Biddy) Walsh, the daughter of the owner of Wheogo Station in 1856.

His first brush with the law came in 1862 when he was arrested at Wowingragong racecourse and charged with armed robbery. When tried for the charge in Orange, the jury acquitted him without leaving the box.

Hall was arrested again several times but never committed because of lack of evidence. Police Inspector, Sir Frederick Pottinger, was the force behind this apparent victimisation.

When Hall returned to his property he found his home burnt down, his cattle dead or strayed and his wife run off with a former policeman named Taylor.

A few weeks later, police saw Hall with one of the Gardiner gang and chased and fired upon him. Desperate and wronged, Hall decided to join the bandits.

Soon after, Gardiner and his men planned their most daring robbery, the hold-up of the gold escort at Eugowra Rocks. It was the afternoon of 15th June, 1862.

The robbery netted the gang more than 14,000 pounds worth of gold dust and currency from a Cobb and Co. coach bound for Sydney. Two of the four troopers escorting the coach were wounded.

Gardiner fled to Queensland and Hall, although arrested, was released when the man who turned Queen's evidence, failed to name him as a gang member. Four of Gardiner's gang were arrested for the robbery – Charters, Bow, Fordyce and Manns. Bow and Fordyce were sentenced to long terms of imprisonment while Manns was executed.

Hall assumed leadership of the gang and under him they carried out many daring exploits . . .

They roamed the countryside from Bathurst to Yass, holding up travellers, banks, stations and mail coaches . . . sometimes working together, sometimes alone.

Ben Hall was always courteous to women, even when robbing them of their jewellery and was never known to have killed anyone, although other members of the gang did so on several occasions.

But Hall's luck ran out on 5th May, 1865. He was betrayed to police by Mick Connolly, who had known the bushranger when he was still a respectable man on the land.

That night Connolly led inspector Davidson, Sergeant Condell, five troopers and a blacktracker to where Hall was sleeping in a gully.

Police decided to wait for dawn before approaching . . . and in the grey light of a new day it was Billy Dargin, the blacktracker, who ended the career of one of Australia's most famous bushrangers.

Once Dargin had killed Hall, the police rushed forward and emptied their guns into the lifeless form. It was said that no less than 36 bullets were found in the body.

Hall's grave lay unmarked in the Forbes cemetery for many years before a plain headstone was erected over the site. The inscription reads: "In memory of Ben Hall, shot 5th May, 1865, aged 27 years".

Who was Ben Hall?

Dangerous outlaw?

. . . Ben Hall was the son of convict parents and was raised in the Murrurundi district. His exact birthplace was never recorded.

When he was about 12 years old, the Hall family moved to the Lachlan district. However, in 1855 or '56, his father and some of the children returned to Murrurundi leaving three of the offspring behind. One was young Ben Hall.

In 1856 Hall married Bridget Walsh at Bathurst. Then in 1860, in partnership with his brother-in-law, John McGuire, he leased Sandy Creek Station in the Weddin Mountains; a run of 16,000 acres.

By 1862 Ben was mixing with many people who lived left of the law and was playing up with several women. It was at this time that his wife, Bridget, left home and went to live with a man named James Taylor. Taylor was also involved with many of the bush criminals.

Within a few months of Bridget leaving him, Hall became mixed up in a robbery, carried out by the Frank Gardiner gang. He and gang member, John Youngman, were arrested by the Inspector in Charge of the Lachlan, Sir Frederick Pottinger, and were committed for trial. However, Youngman skipped bail, leaving Hall to face the music. Fortunately for Hall a witness at the trial changed his story and after retiring for 30 minutes the jury returned a not guilty verdict.

Two months later, Hall joined Gardiner again, and with six other men held up and attacked the Forbes gold escort at Eugowra. Two of the escort troopers were wounded during the attack.

Again arrested, Hall escaped justice when a key witness refused to name Hall as one of the gang members. The witness, Dan Charters, was Hall's best friend and had close associations with the rest of the gang. Of the other gang members, John Bow and Alex Fordyce were sentenced to long terms of imprisonment, while Henry Manns was hanged.

By January, 1863, Ben Hall was up to his neck in crime. He was involved in full time bushranging with Patsy Daley, John O'Meally, John Gilbert and several others.

For the next two and a half years Hall and his cohorts were involved in continual robbery, attempted murder, murder of two policemen and a civilian, wounding tens of people, whippings, arson and kidnapping.

The gang fired on women and children, abused them and used unspeakable language in their presence.

Ben Hall's run of crime came to an end in 1865 when he, Gilbert and John Dunn made plans to visit a harbourer who lived near Billabong Creek, about 12 miles north-west of Forbes.

All the evidence in the archives today points to this person being a man named Strickland, who immediately contacted Sub-inspector Davidson and reported the intended visit.

So on 29th April, the police party left Forbes on what was to be the fateful encounter with the notorious bushranger.

Six days later Ben Hall was shot.

His grave was marked by his family with the traditional paling fence used in that period, but by the early 1900s this had rotted away. Years later the grave was marked with a headstone.

Ways of working

Each of you will be at a different stage in wordprocessing.
This unit is for those of you who have *some* experience of it.

Here are some of the **disadvantages** of writing on a
wordprocessor:

Disadvantages

- *You have no record of the drafts of a piece of writing, so you can't see how your writing evolved.*
- *Pen and paper are still better, because you can compose anywhere and at any time.*
- *The screen is too small, so you can't see a whole piece of work at once and you can't work on the edges of the paper.*
- *You need to be able to type in order to wordprocess well.*

Do you agree?

What are some of the **advantages**, and do they outweigh the
disadvantages? (You could expand this into a full-scale debate or
essay.)

Advantages

If you do have a wordprocessor, or know how to
use a particular wordprocessing program, write
a simple guide or manual to help those in the
class who don't know how to use it.

*For those who don't know how to use a
wordprocessing program,* try out the guides
written by other members of your class. Let
them know if the guides aren't clear and easy to
follow!

Hold the front page!

In pairs or small groups, your job is to create the front page of a newspaper. You will have to make many editorial (and design) decisions as you compose this front page, and the following questions and points are to guide you:

- **Size:** are you going to work to tabloid (A3) or to the size of the 'quality' newspapers (A2)? This may depend on the size of your group.
- **Content:** is your front page going to contain general news, or is it to be from a specialist paper (e.g. sports, fashion, local news, school news)?
- **Audience:** are you aiming it at your friends, your teachers, your parents, or at the wider community? Where is it going to be displayed?
- **Format:** having looked at examples of existing newspapers, how are you going to set out your front page? It may help to make an early sketch of the arrangement of photographs, news stories, advertisements, the title of the newspaper and the main headlines.
- **Responsibilities:** you can also decide at this stage who is going to do what.
- **Timing:** how long have you got to complete this front page? What is your *deadline*?

o O o O o O o O o

Once you have got this far, you will be in a position to start drafting your stories, reports and articles for the page. More questions arise at this stage:

- **Length:** how many words can you fit into the spaces you've allowed for articles?
- **Headlines:** these will be determined by space and the size of your lettering. Are any of the articles to have sub-headings?
- **Research:** how will you find out the information you need to write the reports?
- **Helping each other:** you can act as editors on each other's material, suggesting revisions and other improvements as you go along.

- **Photographs:** On sheets 43B and 43C you will find some photographs that you may be able to use. Other photos can be cut from magazines and newspapers. Remember that you can cut ('crop') the photographs to suit your needs: you may want a particular size to fit a space on your page; or you may want to emphasise some aspect of the photograph to illustrate your written material. Photographs in newspapers usually carry *captions*.

o O o O o O o O o

And when you get to the stage of composing the page itself:

- **Written, typed or wordprocessed?** Use whichever medium suits you best, or is available to you. You might even have access to a program that enables you to compose the page on disc.

On this sheet and the next one is a selection of photographs you might like to use as you compose your front page. You will find others in existing newspapers and magazines.

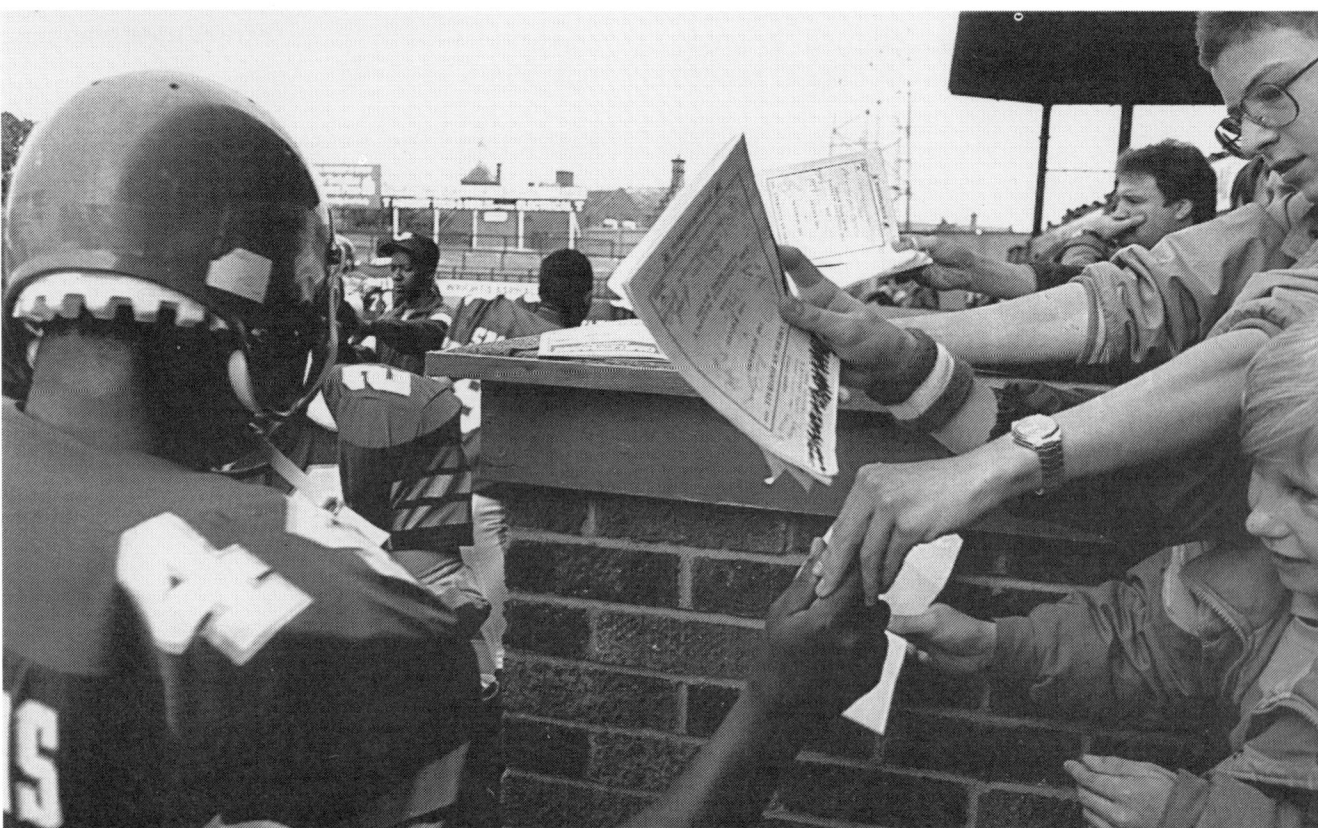

mototrend tyres
TREAD AND SHOULDERS ABOVE THE REST
HOWARTH TIMBER LTD
VIKING HOTEL
F R PULLEYN

Other English Titles from Unwin Hyman

Unwin Hyman Skills and Resources Series

English in Action   Andrew Goodwyn   0 0444 0298 8
English: Skill by Skill   Geoff Barton   0 0444 8104 7
Shakespeare: An Active Approach   Brenda Pinder   0 0444 8159 4

The Unwin Hyman English Series
Unwin Hyman Short Stories
Bright Streets, Dark Corners edited by David Harmer   0 0444   8173 X
Crimebusters edited by Barry Pateman & Jennie Sidney   0 0444 8139 X
Crying for Happiness edited by Jane Leggett   0 0444 8026 1
Dreams and Resolutions edited by Roy Blatchford   0 7135 2841 9
First Class edited by Michael Bennett   0 0444 8105 5
It's Now or Never edited by Jane Leggett & Roy Blatchford   0 7135 2832 X
Openings edited by Roy Blatchford   0 7135 1336 5
Pigs is Pigs edited by Trevor Millum   0 7135 2814 1
Round Two edited by Roy Blatchford   0 7134 2362 X
School's OK edited by Josie Karavasil & Roy Blatchford   0 7135 2450 2
Shorties edited by Roy Blatchford   0 0444 8041 5
Snakes and Ladders edited by H. T. Robertson   0 0444 8004 0
Stepping Out edited by Jane Leggett   0 7135 2712 9
Sweet and Sour edited by Gervase Phinn   0 7135 2713 7
That'll Be The Day edited by Roy Blatchford   0 7135 2711 0

Unwin Hyman Collections
Free As I Know edited by Berverley Naidoo   0 7135 2807 9
Funnybones edited by Trevor Millum   0 0444 0297 X
In Our Image edited by Andrew Goodwyn   0 7135 2856 7
Northern Lights edited by Leslie Wheeler & Douglas Young   0 0444 8127 6
Solid Ground edited by Jane Leggett & Sue Libovitch   0 7135 2842 7

Unwin Hyman Plays
Right on Cue edited by Gervase Phinn   0 0444 8090 3
Scriptz edited by Ian Lumsden   0 0444 8124 1
Stage Write edited by Gervase Phinn   0 7135 2813 3

Writing and Response edited by Roy Blatchford & Jackie Head   0 0444 8093 8
Words – A User's Handbook David Waite   0 0444 8174 8
Poetry Horizons (Volumes 1 and 2) Richard Andrews & Ian Bentley   0 7135 2679 3   0 7135 2680 7
War Poems Christopher Martin   0 0444 8146 2
Changing Islands Eric Boagey   0 7231 0852 8
Poetry Workbook Eric Boagey   0 7135 2804 4
Introducing the Novel Eric Reader & Pamela Woods   0 7135 2752 8
Introducing Dickens John Kassman   0 7135 2788 9
Starting Shakespeare Eric Boagey   0 7135 2753 6
Starting Drama Eric Boagey   0 7135 2681 5